# THREE WISHES

Palestinian
and Israeli
Children Speak

# THREE WISHES

Deborah Ellis

A Groundwood Book
Douglas & McIntyre
Toronto
Vancouver
Berkeley

All images are courtesy of the author except for the following: page 6 © Foundation for Middle East Peace/cartographer Jan de Jong; pages 9, 24, 29, 34, 61, 86, 95 courtesy of Richard Swift; page 22 courtesy of Yad Vashem; page 51 © Dave Bartruff/CORBIS/MAGMA; page 54 AFP/Jaafar Ashtiyeh; page 55 AFP/Fayez Nureldine; page 62 © PENGON; page 71 AFP/Avigail Uzi; page 78 © Reuters NewMedia Inc./CORBIS/MAGMA; page 83 (top) AFP/Eyal Warshavsk; page 88 AFP/Ayman Mansour.

---

Groundwood Books / Douglas & McIntyre
720 Bathurst Street, Suite 500, Toronto, Ontario

Distributed in the USA by Publishers Group West
1700 Fourth Street, Berkeley, CA 94710

We acknowledge for their financial support of our publishing program the Canada Council for the Arts, the Government of Canada through the Book Publishing Industry Development Program (BPIDP), the Ontario Arts Council and the Government of Ontario through the Ontario Media Development Corporation's Ontario Book Initiative.

ONTARIO ARTS COUNCIL
CONSEIL DES ARTS DE L'ONTARIO

National Library of Canada Cataloging in Publication
Ellis, Deborah
Three wishes: Palestinian and Israeli children speak / by Deborah Ellis.
ISBN 0-88899-554-7 (bound).–ISBN 0-88899-645-4 (pbk.)
1. Arab-Israeli conflict–Juvenile literature. I. Title.
DS119.7.E43 2004    j956.04    C2003-906919-2

Printed and bound in Canada

In World War I, 15 percent of all casualties were civilians.
In World War II, 50 percent of all casualties were civilians.
In 2004, 90 percent of casualties in war are civilians.

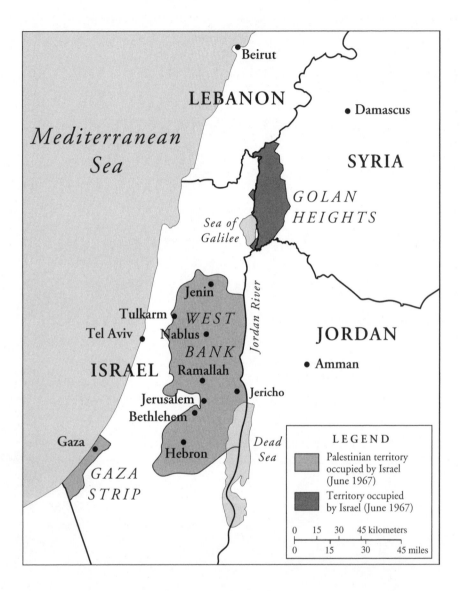

LEGEND

Palestinian territory
occupied by Israel
(June 1967)

Territory occupied
by Israel (June 1967)

0    15    30    45 kilometers

0    15    30    45 miles

# Introduction

The children and young people in this book share a very small piece of land on the Mediterranean Sea. This land, once called Palestine, is a land sacred to Jews, Muslims and Christians, but the area has been at war for more than fifty years.

The genocide that took place during World War II caused many Jews to believe that they could not count on governments in the world to protect them. So they would protect themselves in their own land of Israel, where they could live without fear of persecution or extermination. There was, however, a huge problem. Palestinians, as the Arabs of the land are called, were already living there. Their families had been there for generations, raising crops and livestock, and establishing businesses and cities.

Both Jews and Arabs have deep roots in the area – roots that go back thousands of years. And in the past they have often coexisted peacefully. But problems have arisen in the past hundred years, as Arabs felt that they had a right to the same land that the Jews were claiming for their new state.

In 1947 the United Nations created a plan to separate Palestine into two states – one Jewish and one Arab. The Palestinians and the neighboring Arab countries rejected the plan, but in May 1948, Israel declared its independence, and the Israelis and Palestinians went to war. When the Israeli War of Independence ended, Israel controlled most of Palestine, and many Palestinians became refugees, fleeing to neighboring countries or living in refugee camps on their own land.

More wars took place, culminating in 1967 in the Six Day War, in which Israel occupied the Sinai Peninsula, the Gaza Strip, East Jerusalem, part of Syria and much of Jordan. The end result was that Palestine is now divided between Israel and the two areas (the West Bank and the Gaza Strip) known as the Palestinian territories. Ever since, the UN has called for Israel to withdraw its forces, but the two sides have been unable to agree on how this might happen.

The ongoing fight over this land means the children who live here spend their lives in a place of constant war. Sometimes this means living with explosions, gunfire and the sound of helicopter gun ships overhead. Sometimes it means having friends blown up when they get on a bus.

The war is impossible to escape. It has divided families, turned neighbors into enemies and made innocent people fear each other.

I spent some weeks in Israel and the Palestinian territories in November and December of 2002. The months preceding my visit had seen a number of suicide bombings by Palestinians, and the Israelis had responded by sending their army into Palestinian villages and refugee camps and placing virtually all Palestinians under house arrest or curfew.

The curfew continued, off and on, during my time in the area, limiting my own movement and canceling many of the interviews I had set up before leaving Canada. It was a good lesson on the frustrations faced daily by people living there, when plans made in good faith can be changed in an instant by outside forces.

A view of the land.

I asked the children I met to tell me about their lives, what made them happy, what made them afraid and angry, and how the war has affected them. They told me about their wishes for the future. Some of their stories are hopeful. Some are disturbing, even shocking. But they reflect the world these children live in.

Some of the children I talked with by chance, such as when I stopped in at a McDonald's for a cup of coffee, or visited a hospital. Other children were introduced to me by organizations such as those working against house demolitions or assisting Israeli children traumatized by the violence. All of the children had their parent's or guardian's permission to talk with me. Sometimes that permission was revoked when the grown-ups found out I was interviewing both Israelis and Palestinians. Those children do not, therefore, appear in this book.

The war in the Middle East has been going on for so long, and in so many forms, that it often seems as if it will continue forever. But war, like almost everything else humans do, is a choice. Creating weapons is a choice. Allowing a child to go hungry or to drink poisoned water is a choice. Sitting on the sidelines and doing nothing to stop something that's wrong is a choice.

The children in this book talk about how the choices other people have made have affected their lives. The history of the area and its people is a weight that has been placed, none too gently, on their shoulders.

Deborah Ellis
Toronto, 2004

Since the beginning of the war in the Middle East in 1948, 120,000 people have died. Between September 29, 2000, when the second Intifada, or Palestinian uprising against Israeli occupation, began, and March 7, 2003, 3,399 people were killed. Of these, 429 were children under the age of eighteen.

# Here are their names:

Khalid al-Baziyan, 15
Mohammed Jamal Mohammed al-
Durra, 12
Samer Tabanjah, 12
Iyad Ahmed al-Khashee, 16
Hasan Bakhit, 17
Musleh Abu-Jarad, 17
Wa'el Mohammed Qattawi, 16
Hussam Ismael al-Hamshari, 16
Mohammed Abu-Assi, 12
Majdi Samer Maslamani, 15
Yousef Khalaf, 17
Sami Hassan Salmi, 17
Sami Fathi Abu-Jazar, 12
Moayad Osama Ali Javarish, 14
Ala'a Bassam Bani Nimreh, 13
Samer Iweissi, 15
Tha'er Daoud Mualla, 17
Mohammed Adel Hasan Abu
Tahoun, 16
Omar Ibrahim al-Buheisi, 16
Majib Ibrahim Hawamdeh, 15
Wa'el Hassan a Nashit, 12
Salah Eddin Fawzi Niejem, 15
Sa'ed al-Tanbour, 17

Ashraf Habayeb, 15
Nidal Zudhi al-Dbeiqi, 17
Iyad Sami Sha th, 14
Ala'a Mohammed al-Jawabeh, 14
Bashir Saleh Mousa Selweit, 15
Hussni al-Najjar, 14
Tha'er Ibrahim Abu Zeid, 17
Ahmad Suleiman Abu-Tayeh, 14
Mohammed Hajay, 14
Ibrahim Omar, 14
Yazan Halayquah, 15
Khaled al-Khatib, 17
Rami Ahmad Abdel-Fattah Muae,
15
Maher Mohammed al-Sa'idi, 16
Mohammed Nawaf al-Ta'aban, 17
Wajdi al-Hattab, 13
Fares Odeh, 14
Kalil Abu Sa'ad, 15
Ibrahim Qassas, 13
Raed Dawoud, 14
Mohammed Ghali, 15
Khaled Zahra, 17
Mohammed Abed Sharab, 17
Osama Salem Azouqa, 15

Osama Sameer Jarjawi, 17
Mousa Ibrahim, 14
Bassel Abu Kammer, 15
Mahmoud abu Naji, 15
Yehya Abu Shamaleh, 17
Sabir Barash, 15
Mohammed Khater Mohammed
   Ajleh, 13
Jadua Abu Kbash, 15
Ibrahim Abdel Jaadi, 15
Ahmed Sha'aban, 17
Muhammed Abu Rayan, 16
Abdel Dahshan, 14
Ibrahim Ahmed Othman, 16
Yasser Nabatite, 16
Ibrahim Muqannen, 14
Ayssar Hasseis, 14
Majdi Abed, 15
Mahmoud Mansour Adwan, 16
Mahdi Jaber, 16
Karem el Kurd, 14
Mohammed Abdallah
   Mashharawi, 14
Waleed el Badan, 17
Mohammed el Aya, 12
Medhat Mohammed Jadallah, 14
Mahmoud Yehya, 17
Amar Samir Mashni, 16
Mu'ataz Telakh, 16
Salim Mohammed Hamaydeh, 12
Ahmed Qawasmi, 14
Mohammed Amin Mohammed
   Daoud, 17
Hani al-Soufi, 14
Arafat Jabarin, 17
Mu'ath Ahmed Hadwan, 12
Benyamin Bergman, 15
Ofir Rahum, 16
Shalhevet Pass, 10 months
Eliran Rosenberg-Zayat, 15

Naftali Lanzkorn, 13
Yossi Ish-Ran, 14
Kobi Mendell, 14
Marina Berkowizki, 17
Anya Kazachkov, 16
Katherine Kastaniyade-Talkir, 15
Alesksei Lupalu, 16
Mariana Medvedenko, 15
Irina Nepomneschi, 16
Yulia Nelimov, 16
Raisa Nimrovsky, 15
Liana Sakiyan, 16
Maria Tagilchev, 14
Avraham Nahman Nitzani, 17
Yevgenia Dorfman, 15
Yehuda Shoham, 5 months
Ronen Landau, 17
Michal Raziel, 16
Malka Roth, 15
Raiaya Schijveschuurder, 14
Avraham Yitzhak Schiveschuurder,
   4
Hemda Schijveschuurder, 2
Tamara Shimashvili, 8
Jocheved Shoshan, 10
Aliza Malka, 17
Shoshana Ben Ishai, 16
Menashe Regev, 14
Assaf Avitan, 15
Israel Ya'akov Danino, 17
Yair Amar, 13
Golan Turgeman, 15
Adam Weinstein, 14
Ido Cohen, 17
Omar Khaled Farouq, 10
Mohammed Sharef, 15
Safwat Isam Qeshtah, 16
Issa Ibrahim El Amori, 14
Ahmed Abdel Razek Abu Huli, 15
Hussan Imad El Diesi, 15

Obi Mohammed Daraj, 9
Mohammed Malmoud Halss, 13
Murtaja Amir, 17
Mahmoud Aldrawesh, 11
Yehya Fathi el Sheikh Eid, 12
Mahmoud Abu Sheihadeh, 16
Ahmed Maraheil, 16
Lo'ay el Tamimi, 11
Ahmed el Assar, 16
Sawkat Hassan Alami, 14
Hamzah Khader Obed, 14
Rami Mousa Ghareb, 16
Bara el Sha'er, 10
Mohamad Mhareb, 11
Iman Hameed Hijo, 4 months
Hussam Tafesh, 16
Mohammed Salem, 15
Ala Adel e Buji, 15
Ahmed Saleh Abu el Helou, 17
Ali Abu Shaweish, 10
Adel Muqannen, 16
Ahmed Yassin, 15
Murad Al Masri, 14
Khalil Ibrahim Al Mughrabi, 11
Tariq Abu Dab at, 17
Rifa Al Nahal, 15
Bilal Abdel Mun'em, 9
Ashraf Abdel Mun'em, 6
Muhamad Subhi Abu Arar, 13
Enas Zeid, 7
Muhamad Al-Ajouz, 15
Ibrahim Saraf, 14
Tamer Riyad Zo'rab, 17
Mohammed Samer Abu-Libdeh, 15
Balqees Fathi Al-qaida, 12
Ramzi Khalel Hasoneh, 17
Emad Atta Zo'roub, 15
Mahmoud Jalal Qeshta, 16
Mo'aweya Ali Alnahal, 14

Mohamed Fathi Altarayera, 10
Mahmoud Ali Soukar, 16
Musen Fahed Arar, 17
Reham Abu Elward, 10
Basel Elmobasher, 13
Yousef Abayaat, 15
Ahmad Yousef Abu Mandeel, 17
Naseer Hani Qur'an, 13
Fouad Al Dahshan, 17
Ahmad abu Mustafa, 13
Mohammed Naem Kareem Al-Astal, 13
Akram Naem Mohammed Al-Astal, 6
Anees Edrees Mohammed Al-Astal, 10
Omar Edrees Mohammed Al-Astal, 12
Mohammed Sultan Mohammed Al-Astal, 11
Wael Ali Radwan, 15
Aayat Al-Akhras, 17
Kefah Khaled Ebeed, 14
Mohammed Abu Marsa, 15
Borham Ibrahem Al Hemoni, 3
Shadi Ahmad Arafeh, 13
Ahmmed Al-Masri, 15
Yousef Al Najar, 11
Ammar Mohammed Al Ghaleth, 16
Yaseer Sami Al Kasbeh, 11
Mohammed Jam'an Hnedeq, 12
Ahmad Mohammed Banat, 15
Mohammed Ahmad Lbed, 16
Mohammed Al-Madhoun, 16
Nehemia Amar, 15
Rachel Thaler, 16
Liran Nehmad, 3
Lidor Ilan, 12
Ya'akov Avraham, 7 months

Avia Malka, 9 months
Rachel Levy, 17
Adi Shiran, 17
Elmar Dezhabrielov, 16
Netanel Riachi, 17
Avraham Siton, 17
Hadar Hershkowitz, 14
Galila Bugala, 11
Neria Shabo, 16
Avishai Shabo, 5
Sarah Tiferet Shilon, 8 months
Osnat Abramov, 16
Hadas Turgeman, 14
Hodaya Asraf, 13
Yafit Ravivo, 14
Noy Anter, 12
Gavriel Hoter, 17
Yael Ohana, 11
Karen Shatsky, 15
Shiraz Nehmad, 7
Shaul Nehmad, 15
Oriah Ilan, 18 months
Avraham Eliahu Nehmad, 7
Atara Livne, 15
Gal Ron, 15
Danielle Shefi, 5
Sinai Keinan, 5 months
Gilad Stiglitz, 14
Adi Dahan, 17
Shani Avi-Zedek, 15
Gal Eisenman, 5
Zvika Shabo, 12
Yonatan Gamliel, 16
Linoy Saroussi, 14
Gaston Perpinal, 15
Ilan Perlman, 8
Michael Sharshevsky, 16
Dvir Anter, 14
Mohammed Ali Joudeh, 16
Samer Sami Alkasbeh, 15

Lo'ai Mohammed Adeli, 15
Fadi Al'Azizi, 16
Samir Abu Myala, 13
Mas'od Abu Jalal, 17
Muna al-Ja'aysah, 10
Mohammed al-Nims, 17
Nurah Jamal Shalhub, 16
Lu'ay Thabaiah, 16
Mahmoud al-Talalqah, 7
Inas Ibrahim Salah, 9
Ahmad Hashash, 15
Bara Abu Kwaik, 17
Mohammed Abu Kwaik, 8
Arafat al-Masri, 7
Sa'ed Ali Subaih, 16
Shayma Emad Al-Masri, 7
Yousef Shihada, 17
Tariq Abu Jamoos, 17
Mahmoud Ma'moun al'Bitar, 9
Sayyed Faiz Abu Sayfein, 14
Mahmoud Tayseer Ghanim, 15
Rawan al-Jabrini, 15
Amani al Awawdah, 16
Salem al Awawdah, 9
Tariq al Awawdah, 8
Sha'ima Sa'yed Hamad, 11
Mujahied Abu Shabab, 2
Mohammed al-Maghibi, 10
Riham Abu Taha, 4
Mahmoud Abu Yasien, 13
Hamadah Akram al-Siqali, 14
Khaled Ra'rour, 17
Faiz Khaled Salah, 13
Issa Da'doub, 15
Hani Abu Irmali, 16
Mohammed Hawashien, 13
Dina Sawaftah, 13
Rubien Jamil al-Khadour, 15
Salwa Hamed Dahliez, 12
Sumaya Najieh Hassan, 6

Esra Othman, 10
Asad Faisal Qarini, 10
Saed Subhi al-Wahesh, 10
Amjad Ahmad Abdah, 11
Mofasim Rahal, 16
Ahied Abu Ebad, 5
Abdallah al-Shabi, 8
Azam al-Shabi, 7
Anass al-Shabi, 4
Qussi Farah Abu Eishah, 12
Haitham Abu Shouqa, 16
Mahmoud Fadel Abu Zahriah, 9
Tabaruk Jaber Odeh, 4
Ali Qashier, 14
Mahmoud Abu Shawqa, 15
Farah Hikmat Adwan, 4
Amyn Ziad Thawabta, 13
Anwar Hamduna, 13
Yousef Basseil Zakut, 14
Ismail Abu Nadi, 13
Assad Faisal Assan, 12
Eman Mohammed Abu Khousa,
    17
Osama al-Jabarien, 16
Huda Abu Shalof, 2
Abed Ismail, 11
Fadi Hassan al-Ajlouni, 7
Tamar Abu-Serrieh, 9
Majdi Mohammed Ibrahim, 17
Salem Sami el-Shaer, 15
Mohsen Atiyeh Jabr, 17
Ameed Abu-Seer, 7
Mohammed Talal Kassab, 17
Habash Sameer Hanani, 17
Murad Abu Alkam, 16
Ali'abu Sitta, 17
Jamil Abu Aziza, 12
Ahmed Yousef Abu Aziza, 6
Firas Hussam al-Sadi, 13
Sujoud Ahmad Turki Fihmawi, 6

Abdel Shamlakh, 10
Bassam al-Sady, 7
Mohammed Ayesh, 17
Mohammed Ahmad Mubark, 14
Nour al-Hindy, 2
Shukri Fa'ed Abdel-Haj, 6
Moen Ali Al-Adini, 13
Ahmad Jawad Abu-Radaha, 13
Iman Shihada, 15
Ayman Matar, 18 months
Mohammed Matar, 4
Diana Matar, 5
Subhi al-Huwaiti, 4
Mohammed al-Huwaiti, 6
Ahmad al-Shawa, 6
Alaa' Mohammed Matar, 5
Dina Matar, 2 months
Saed Hanani, 17
Niveen Silmi, 3
Asma Ahmad, 9
Hamza Dweekat, 13
Adel Ghiben, 17
Ayman Basem Fares, 5
Ayman Zo'roub, 15
Mohammed Abu Odah, 14
Nihad Othman al-Hajeen, 17
Abdel-Hadi al-Hamaideh, 13
Bahira Daraghmeh, 6
Osama Daraghmeh, 8
Sari Suban, 15
Yazan Abdel Razeq, 15
Abdel Sadi, 16
Abdel Hamail, 10
Abdel Salam al-Gharbali, 14
Waled al-Mghani, 14
Gharam Mana, 14
Rami Barbari, 10
Mahmoud al-Zaghloul, 10
Mohammed Zaid, 16
Ammar Rajab, 16

Ahman Al-Astal, 17
Mohammed al-Astal, 15
Maisa Imad-Zanoun, 12
Mohammed Asher, 16
Ihab Al-Mughair, 17
Thaer al-Hut, 12
Tawfic Braikeh, 4
Shayma Shamalah, 7
Mohammed Hilal, 12
Ahmad Abu Jafar, 12
Mahmoud Abu Mour, 16
Salem Al Shaer, 13
Fouad Abu Ghali, 15
Ahmad Anbass, 16
Eyad Abu Tah, 17
Nafeth Khaled Mashal, 2
Mohammed Abu Al Nijah, 8
Hammed Asad Al-Masri, 4
Mohammed Taher Iwajan, 17
Omran Moustafa, 17
Ibrahim Al Sadie, 17
Eihab Al Zaqleh, 15
Amrou Al Qudsi, 15
Mohammed Balalou, 11
Abed Allah Al Natsheh, 16
Jehad Al Faqih, 8
Abbas Al Atrash, 3
Hatem Rizek Al Agaleh, 16
Mo'ataz Kamal Odeh, 16
Jawad Zidan, 15
Ala'a Alsadodi, 15
Nada Madi, 15
Hanin Abu Sillah, 13
Mohammed Fekr Braik, 14
Abed Salameh, 8
Imran Abu Hamdeyah, 16
Kamar Abu Hamed, 12

Smadar Firstater, 16
Daniel Haroush, 16
Tom Hershko, 15
Tal Kerman, 17
Yuval Mendelevitch, 13
Elizabeth Katzman, 16
Abigail Litle, 14
Azzaf Tzur, 17
Mohammed Dawas, 16
Tareq Dawas, 15
Jehad Abed, 15
Tareq Abu Jado, 15
Mohammed Kawarea, 15
Iyad Abu Sa'er, 12
Haza'a Al Afifi, 17
Khaled Salouf, 17
Ali Taleb Aziz, 7
Amjad Al Hatab, 16
Sami Azurba, 17
Mostafa Odwan, 10
Hassan Goul, 8
Adnan Besharat, 13
Ahmad Zahra, 17
Ahmad Afanah, 17
Bara'a Al Afifi, 17
Mohamad Al Kahlut, 15
Mahmoud Zaherah, 14
Nasser Ja'ara, 14
Ahmad Abou Olwan, 13
Abed Jad Allah, 9
Tariq Sadi Aqel, 13
Ehab Nabahat, 14
Mohammed Jamal Mohsen, 14
Thaer Rehan, 13
Tarek Al Najar, 14
Imzeh Jabrel Farmot, 17
Baker Saeed Hawash, 15

# THREE WISHES

Palestinian
and Israeli
Children Speak

## Artov, 15

In the late 1800s and early 1900s, long before the state of Israel was created, many Jewish immigrants came to Palestine from Russia and Eastern Europe. These immigrants were seeking a place where they could live as Jews, away from the anti-Semitism and persecution that plagued them. Many had lost everything in the pogroms, which were campaigns to destroy Jewish communities. Under the Russian tsar, pogroms were commonplace, but even after the tsar was overthrown in the Russian Revolution in 1917,  the Communist regime frequently targeted Jews for abusive treatment. Today, many Jews still move to Israel because of the anti-Semitism in their home countries.

Israel's policy is that any Jewish person has the right to live there. The government encourages immigration, and Israeli society is a mixture of people who are born in the area and those who have come from more than eighty other countries. When these people move to Israel, they are given help to learn Hebrew and to otherwise settle in.

Artov is a recent arrival in Israel. He is touring Yad Vashem, the Holocaust Memorial Museum in Jerusalem. Footpaths through the 45-acre park join the museums, art galleries and monuments that commemorate the six million Jews killed by the Nazis.

I have been in Israel only three months. I am from Russia. I miss Russia very much, even though Israel is very beautiful. I especially miss the food. My favorite food is plov, a special dish from Uzbekistan. There are a lot of Russians in Israel, so I can get Russian food here, but it doesn't taste the same as it does at home.

I came to Israel with my family. I have one sister. She is

older. Sometimes she is nice, sometimes she is tiresome. She likes being here, but I think she also misses being at home.

My parents wanted to come here. They wanted to live as Jews in Israel. Even though they loved their home in Russia, they still wanted to be in Israel. A lot of Jews have left Russia and come here.

Russia hasn't liked Jews. Many Jews have been killed there. My grandparents told me about the pogroms, where Jews would be driven from their homes and killed, just because they were Jews. That's why a lot of Russian Jews moved to Israel, so they would have a place where they could live and be safe. Even nowadays, it is not very safe to be a Jew in Russia. We hear stories on the news. Some people put up big signs along the roads. The signs say "Death to Jews," and "Jews are garbage." When someone tries to take them down, the signs blow up, because they have a bomb attached. Jewish cemeteries in Russia have been destroyed, too, and rabbis have been beaten up.

We live in Netanya now. It is on the Mediterranean Sea, north of Tel Aviv. It is lovely to live near the sea, and it is warmer here than in Russia. I like school. It makes me happy to see and learn new things. Phys ed is my favorite subject. I also love playing computer games, particularly one called Dragon.

I came to Yad Vashem today with my teacher. It is a place where Jews who were killed in the Holocaust are remembered. We have been to all the buildings, and now we are in the Historical Museum. This is the last building to see. There are glass cases on the bottom floor of this building with toys children played with in the concentration camps – dolls made out of straw, things like that. Seeing them made me think of what I would play with if I'd been in a camp.

This whole place is like a park. Trails lead through trees

Statues on top of the Children's Memorial at Yad Vashem.

from one building to another. Each building is for a different type of memory. The Hall of Remembrance is a big room with a fire burning all the time in the middle of it. On the floor around the fire are the names of the camps where Jews died. The Hall of Names lists the people who were killed.

There is also an old train car, the kind used to ship cattle to the slaughterhouse. This one was used to ship Jews to the camps. It's up on a railway bridge, but the bridge stops, and the car is right on the edge, with nowhere to go.

I feel very Jewish being here, like I am connected to these people, even though my life is very different from the way theirs was. I understand a little better just why my parents wanted to move here.

The Children's Memorial was the hardest to see. You go into it the way you go into a cave. When you first go in, everything is dark and silent. You follow a path, holding onto ropes, until you start to see the lights.

Small candles are lit everywhere, reflected over and over in mirrors, so that it looks like the little lights go on and on. The lights stand for the Jewish children who were killed by the Nazis. The lights look like stars. Above, through a speaker, a quiet voice reads out the names and ages of the children who were murdered.

I can't talk about this anymore just now. I will cry if I do.

Before we moved to Israel, we heard about the war that is going on here now. We knew it would be dangerous, but we wanted to come anyway.

I will become a citizen of Israel and so I will serve in the army. It scares me a bit, thinking of becoming a soldier. We see on the television the terrible dangers soldiers are in. It is frightening what people can do to each other. When I finish with the army, I want to be a veterinarian, or a magician.

I know a little bit about the Palestinians from the news. It seems that they all hate us, but I don't know why. I have not met any yet. It is impossible for us to meet. We are separate people.

My teacher says that two years ago there were a lot of Palestinian students in Israel. She says it was good when Jews and Palestinians could meet and get to know each other a bit, so they wouldn't be afraid of each other. But they don't come into Israeli territory anymore. Now it is too dangerous for them to come. The Jewish people will think they are terrorists, and their own people will think they are traitors. So they stay with their own people, and we stay with ours.

## Nora, 12

**Nora is a student at the Princess Basma Rehabilitation Centre for Disabled Children. This is a school where children can receive both an academic education and special treatment for their disabilities. It sits on the top of the Mount of Olives, a high hill overlooking the Old City of Jerusalem. The halls and classrooms of the large white cement building are designed to make it easy for the children to move around on**  **crutches and wheelchairs. The children use their various abilities to help each other down hallways or out to the playground — pushing wheelchairs or providing a stronger shoulder to lean on.**

**Nora's classroom is down a long ramp to the basement.**

I am from Beit Safafa, to the south of Jerusalem, in Palestinian territory. I am a Palestinian.

I have three brothers, but no sister. I wish I did have a sister. I sometimes think about all the things we could do and talk about. If she were close to my age, we could wear each other's clothes. Then it would be like we had twice as many clothes. My brothers are nice, but they are all younger than me, and they can be very noisy. They bother me sometimes. Of course, I bother them right back, but because I'm the oldest, I'm supposed to be better behaved. At least I have my own room. Pink is my favorite color, so I have a lot of pink in my room.

I love my brothers, but they can sometimes give me problems, like the day when I went to shop by myself. I was born with something wrong with my legs. I've always been in a wheelchair. I get around in the chair just fine. The wheels are like my legs.

I'm not supposed to go out by myself because my mother

thinks I won't be able to move fast enough if the soldiers come. There are a lot of soldiers where I live. They watch us all the time. We can't do anything without being watched by them. They carry guns, and they give me nightmares. We would like them to go away, but they don't care about what we want.

The soldiers are always around, but sometimes they move into the streets, and then everybody runs to get out of their way. If they feel like shooting, they will just go ahead and shoot. They don't care if they shoot at a child or an older person.

My mother is afraid they will shoot at me for not getting out of their way fast enough. I think I could throw stones like the other children and still get away quickly, but I can't throw stones if I'm with my mother.

The streets aren't always smooth, though. Sometimes there are a lot of rough places where the army has blown something up. I can't move my chair on my own over places like that. Someone has to push me. My mother doesn't allow me to go out by myself, but I went anyway one day when she wasn't paying attention.

It was fun to be out by myself. I felt scared that she would

A view of the Old City of Jerusalem from the Mount of Olives.

catch me, but it was an adventure, too. I felt brave and scared at the same time.

I went to a little shop not far from our house. I bought some chewing gum. My mother doesn't like me to have chewing gum, either, but I like it, so that's what I bought.

I made it back home without being caught. Everything would have been fine, but then I told my oldest brother what I had done. I wanted to brag, I guess. My brother thinks he's so great. I should have known better. He went and told on me to my mother. She lectured me in front of him, about how I should be smarter than that and set a good example for my younger brothers. I didn't like that, but I did like the gum.

I'm usually late for school, but that doesn't have anything to do with me being in a wheelchair. There's a van that goes to the Palestinian towns and camps and picks up kids like me to come to the school here. We're supposed to be let through the checkpoints because we have a special permit. Even if there is a curfew on, we are supposed to be able to get through, but the soldiers always hold us up. Even though they know us, even though they see the same faces every morning, they still ask for our identification papers. They count all the kids and ask us a lot of questions. They don't care if we're late for school or not.

Many of the kids in my class come late. School is supposed to start at eight-thirty, but kids come in at all times during the morning. It's hard to concentrate with kids coming in all the time. The teachers are often late, too.

We're celebrating Ramadan now. We fast during the day. Not all Palestinians are Muslims, but my family is. At the end of Ramadan, we celebrate Eid. Eid is a wonderful holiday, and I can't wait. First I will go to the mosque with my mother and we will pray together. Then we will go to visit other members of our family.

We can't go to visit my grandparents, though. They live in

a town in the West Bank, and the Israelis won't let us go through the checkpoints to visit them. They live so close to us, just a few miles, but they might as well live far, far away. That's what would make me the happiest, to see my grandparents again. I haven't seen them in over two years.

I don't know any Israeli people other than soldiers, and they are all very mean and very tough. The children are probably the same as the adults. They might be nice like me at the beginning, but they would change. They want our land, and that makes them mean.

I know there are other children in the world who suffer a lot. They get shot at even more than we do, and they get sick and go hungry. Some day I'd like to do something to help them. If I had three wishes I would become a doctor and I would be famous, maybe as a writer. And I would be able to walk.

# Talia, 16

When the state of Israel was first created, many people lived in kibbutzim — collectively run communities. People in a kibbutz held property in common and worked together for the good of the community and for the good of Israel. This was a way to build Israel, and it was a way of stating that there was value in putting the needs of the country and the community first.

Israeli youth are still raised to have a strong sense of obligation to the state of Israel, and to the community of Judaism. Membership in youth groups, both religious and secular, is encouraged, so that young people feel part of a larger community. Youth groups stress service to others, gaining skills, recreation and appreciation of history.

Talia lives near Emek Refain, a street in West Jerusalem full of boutiques, coffee houses and little shops. West Jerusalem is in Israeli territory. It is a very new, modern city that sprawls west from the Old City. It has beautiful homes, parks and tree-lined streets.

I am in the eleventh grade at school. My best subject is Hebrew literature. I'm a good student. My friends take school seriously, too. The thing I like doing the most is hanging out in coffee shops with my friends, but the war makes it difficult for us to do that. We can't go downtown or to a mall, because we are afraid about what could happen. We could be sitting in a café, just talking normally, and we could be blown up in the middle of a conversation. My mother worries a lot. Bombs go off when nobody expects them to.

I know a girl whose sister was killed when she was out buying books for school. She was only sixteen, the same age I am now. This was a few years ago. Death can come for us any-

Downtown in West Jerusalem.

where, any time. It doesn't matter if you are ready for it or not.

It isn't safe to be Jewish here, but it has never been safe to be Jewish anywhere. At least we can protect ourselves here, because this is our country.

I went to Poland recently with the Scouts. We spent two months studying before we went. We attended seminars, listened to speakers and had activities and discussions. We learned which countries were involved in World War II, the issues involved, things like that, as well as learning about what happened to the Jews.

We had already been on field trips to the Holocaust Memorial, Yad Vashem, but the purpose of the trip to Poland was to see for ourselves what happened to the Jews during the war. Many people here in Israel have relatives who were killed by the Nazis. Many of the older citizens of Israel have numbers tattooed on their arms, which shows they were in the concentration camps. This trip was to show us the places where these terrible things happened, and to help us to understand ourselves and our people better.

We traveled all over Poland. We went to Warsaw and saw where the Jewish ghetto used to be. Jews fought the Nazis there, until the Nazis killed many of them and shipped the rest of them off to the concentration camps.

We also went to Auschwitz. This was one of the places where Jews were sent to be killed. We saw the hair that had been cut from the Jews' heads, and the shoes that had been taken from their feet. We saw the gas chambers where they were killed. These were big shower rooms. Jews would be forced to go in there, many at a time, men, women and children together, all naked, as though they were going to have a shower. Out of the shower heads came poison gas instead of water, and killed everyone in the room. We saw hairbrushes, hand mirrors, jewelry, eyeglasses, suitcases, books, menorahs – things that were special to their families. These things were all taken away from them as soon as they came into the camp.

When you enter Auschwitz, you can imagine being a Jew sixty years ago, walking into the camp, with police dogs barking, and German soldiers hitting you with their rifles, and everyone scared and crying. It was snowing when we were there. We were all dressed in layers of clothing, and so we were warm. When Jews were prisoners there, they had no warm clothes, or boots, or blankets, or enough food.

Most of the camp is still there – the barracks where prisoners were crammed together, the guard towers, the other buildings. As I walked around, I tried to feel what they would have felt, but of course I couldn't.

It was amazing to be walking around with the flag of Israel. The Nazis tried to exterminate us, but we survived, and now we have our own country and our own flag. We are here, but the Nazis are not. We did a short, special ceremony at each place and sang the Israeli anthem. I like to think that the ghosts of the people who were murdered there could hear us singing, and that it brought them some peace.

We all went over there thinking we'd come back understanding everything, understanding how such a thing could have happened. But it's too big. I don't know if anybody can ever understand it. It does help to have been there, to be able to visualize the places and imagine a little clearer what those people went through.

It shows that we have to take care of ourselves, that we have to be very serious about our security.

The neighborhood I live in is full of memorials to people who have been killed by the Palestinians. There are little parks and benches dedicated to this person or that person who was killed. It's very weird when I think about it. You know these things happen, but you never think they'll happen close to you.

It's complicated, about the Palestinians. No one seems to have the right answer. It's hard for both sides to come together. It will be even harder soon, because of the wall that's being built around the West Bank. The wall is going to keep the Palestinians out of Israel so they can't bomb us.

It's normal for me to see a lot of soldiers in the streets. My sister's husband comes from the United States, and he said it was hard for him to see so many people walking around with guns. That's a funny thing for him to say, since we learned in school that many more people are killed by guns in the United States than here, and there's a war going on here. He says we should never become used to seeing guns, but I'm used to it already. It would seem strange for me not to see them.

Besides, the soldiers do an important job. Recently, a guard stopped a restaurant from being bombed.

As soon as I finish school, I will go into the army. It's very important to do this, even for girls. It's part of my duty of being an Israeli. I don't support people who don't do their duty, just so they can get on with their lives, without their lives being interrupted. I can understand people being against the war, but if that is how they feel, they can do National Service instead.

It's not possible for someone like me, or my friends, to go into Palestinian-controlled areas. It's too dangerous. If I won't go to my own downtown, I certainly won't go into the West Bank!

I don't know any Palestinian or Arab kids. I don't know if Palestinian kids are like me or not. I don't know anything about them, even how they are living, although I know their living conditions are not good.

I know that I am an Israeli citizen, with equal rights to other Israeli citizens. The Palestinians aren't. They have their own government, but Israel is over everything. The Palestinians aren't allowed to do the things I'm allowed to do, like move around the country.

We have gates around our school that are locked so no one can get in who isn't supposed to be there. There can't be any cars parked around the school. Often when I walk past parked cars along the street, I wonder if one will blow up beside me.

I know a lot of people who have been killed in the war.

A girl from my dance school was killed when a bomb blew up the bus she was riding on. We took a folk dancing class together. I saw her a lot. After the bombing, we did a dance recital in a theater in Jerusalem and dedicated it to her.

I know someone else, a man, he went into the bank, took out some money, walked away down the street, and the street blew up behind him.

My brother's friend, a woman, wore a medallion around her neck, from India. Schrapnel from a bomb hit the medallion instead of her, and she didn't get hurt.

You never know when a bomb will explode. You could be in a bad mood or a good mood, in trouble or doing what you're supposed to do. It doesn't help to lead a good life. Well, it's important to lead a good life, but being good doesn't protect you from the bombs.

The thing that frightens me the most is the thought that something bad could happen to anyone close to me or my family.

The thing that makes me the happiest is when the whole

family comes together. I have a brother who lives in New York, and a sister who lives in Miami. I love seeing them, although my brother used to annoy me a lot when he lived here. He'd kick me out of the room when his friends came over.

We used to go to Sinai for holidays. That was our relaxation. We'd go with our family and friends, but we don't go anymore. It's not safe. There's nowhere to go now that's safe.

Everyone carries a cell phone here. I call Mom a lot, just to say I'm okay, I'm here. If she doesn't hear from me in awhile, she worries that something bad has happened to me. When a big terror attack happens, the phone system breaks down because everyone is trying to call everyone, to make sure they're okay.

I just went camping in the south of Israel with the Scouts for three days, to get a break from everything. We camped in the desert. My friends and I walked a lot. Everything was quiet. The sands were amazingly colorful. It was good to be quiet and away from pressures. The north of Israel is beautiful, too. It's all green and has lots of water.

It would be good for me to meet some Palestinians. Kids are the same everywhere. It's hard for me to think of them as being the same as me, though, because I have a friend in the army. He tells me scary things. A friend of his was killed protecting Jews in a settlement.

For this war to end, everyone will have to give up a little. No one will win completely. It will have to end some day, but both sides will have to give up something.

The world isn't perfect. We should have learned more from the Holocaust – the world, I mean. We didn't learn enough, or the world would be better than it is.

My three wishes? I have just one. I want the war to end, so I can keep living in Israel and raise my children here.

# Michael, 11

Jerusalem is one of the oldest continually inhabited cities in the world. People have lived here since 3000 B.C. Over the centuries the area has had many rulers including Hebrews (Israelites), Babylonians, Persians, Greeks, Romans, Egyptians, crusaders, Arabs, Turks and British.

The Old City of Jerusalem is a world unto itself. It is surrounded by high stone walls with a pathway on top called the Ramparts Walk, which people can still walk on. The city is accessible by very grand gates or entranceways, and it has narrow streets that criss-cross each other like a maze. It is a glorious place to get lost in. Open-fronted shops selling fruit, baked goods, toys, clothes, medicines, and everything else spill onto the streets. Sensations pile upon sensations. You can smell bread baking and kebabs grilling and hot pastries being spread with honey. Fruit and vegetables make brilliant splashes of color against the old stone walls. Fabrics rain down over the pathways, music blares out from the CD stalls, and souvenir shops sell everything from wooden camels to embroidery. And everywhere, there is history.

The Old City is divided into four quarters — the Christian Quarter, the Armenian Quarter, the Jewish Quarter and the Muslim Quarter. It is full of places and memories that are sacred to Judaism, Christianity and Islam, and all three religions consider Jerusalem a holy site. Three of the most revered holy places in the world are contained within the Old City walls — the Church of the Holy Sepulchre, where Jesus was crucified and entombed; the Western Wall (also called the Wailing Wall), the site of the Jewish Holy Temple, where Jews from all over the world come to pray; and the Dome of the Rock, where Muhammad ascended to heaven.

Michael, a Palestinian Christian, lives in an orphanage in the Christian Quarter.

The Old City of Jerusalem.

I am a Palestinian Christian. Many Palestinians are Muslims, and many of us are Christians. It doesn't matter what religion we are. We are all Palestinians.

I live in the Terra Sancta Boys Home in the Old City of Jerusalem, near the New Gate. It's called the New Gate, but it's very old. It's not as old as the Damascus Gate, though, which is close to here as well.

This home is upstairs in a building that's part of a big Catholic church. You can get to the church without going outside, if you know the way.

The Terra Sancta Boys Home is run by monks. It's a home for boys who don't have parents, or who have parents who can't take care of them. I don't have a mother, but I do have a father. He's in America and can't take care of me or my brothers and sisters right now. I miss him. Maybe he'll come to see me at Christmas.

Not all of the boys here are Palestinians, but they are all Christians. One of the boys comes from Russia. He doesn't talk much. I think he misses his home.

I lived in America for a little while. I liked it, especially the snow. I would like to live in a place where there is a lot of snow. We get snow sometimes in Jerusalem, but not like in America. The snow here goes away soon after it hits the ground.

I have been in this home for two and a half years. I have three brothers and one sister. They are all smaller than me. They live with the nuns in a children's home on the Mount of Olives, outside the Old City walls. When my brothers get bigger, they will join me here. My sister will stay with the nuns or go to another home that's just for girls. Sometimes I get to go to the Mount of Olives to see them.

The Mount of Olives is a very holy place for Christians. The Garden of Gethsemane is there, where Jesus prayed before the Romans crucified him. Jerusalem is full of holy places, like the place where Mary was born, and the places where Jesus carried the cross and was crucified. We go to visit these places sometimes on little trips with the monks. We can walk there. The Old City is not very big, and the streets are too narrow for most cars.

There is a procession every Friday through the Old City, along the Via Dolorosa, which means the Street of Sorrows. It passes all the Stations of the Cross, like where Jesus was sentenced to death, and whipped, and where he fell, and where a woman offered him water. Sometimes we go on the procession with the monks, but not every week.

All of us boys sleep together in one big room called the dormitory. I have my own bed and a place to keep my things. We are together all the time, so we are a little bit like a family. Sometimes we argue about things like pocket money or just silly things. Sometimes if someone is feeling sad or lonely, it's easy to start an argument, because that makes you forget what you're feeling.

We have a daily routine here. The monks wake us up at six, and we get dressed, make our beds and tidy the dormitory. After that, we have breakfast. There are nuns who prepare food for us. Breakfast is usually bread, jam and cheese. Then we have jobs to do, like washing the floor or sweeping the stairs. If we do a good job, the Brothers are happy, and I like it when they think I've done well. Sometimes I pretend I'm doing a chore for my father, and that he'll check it and be pleased with me.

We play a lot of games here. In the recreation room, the Brothers put out a big puzzle with hundreds and hundreds of pieces. We all work on that from time to time, trying to fit the pieces together. I love computer games, too, especially one called Jack and Dexter. It's on Play Station Two.

We all take turns being altar boys in the big church here. There are several jobs, like carrying the cross or the incense, and assisting the priest at the altar. There was a lot to learn at first, but it isn't hard. You have to behave during mass, though. No fooling around. Mass is pretty solemn, and if you keep your mind on what you're doing, you don't feel like fooling around.

We go to school here in the home. The Brothers teach us. English is my favorite subject. I'm an okay student. When I grow up, I would like to be a taxi driver, because then I could get into my taxi and go anywhere.

On holidays, we get to sleep in. If I'm here over Christmas, if my father doesn't come to get me, I may sleep in until ten or eleven. I hope my father comes, though. He sent me a toy car for my birthday.

I don't know very much about the war, other than that it means the Palestinians have to live apart from each other. My family isn't the only one that is split up. Families should be together, or should at least be able to visit each other whenever they want to, but that's not the way it is for most Palestinian families. We all seem to be separated from each other because we can't cross the roadblocks.

Sometimes when I'm out walking, or in church, I see families where everyone is together, and my inside aches.

I have never met any Jewish boys. I see them in the streets when we go out of the home. Some of them wear dark clothes and black hats and have hair that hangs down in front of their ears. They are called Hasidic Jews. Not all Jews dress like that.

When I see Jewish boys my age, they look at me, and I look at them, but we don't say anything. I don't know anything about them, and they don't know anything about me.

Sometimes they don't look at me. Sometimes I am too busy thinking of other things to look at them.

We hear a little bit about the fighting between the Israelis and the Palestinians, but I don't really know what's going on, or why they are fighting. I wish the fighting would stop because I don't like the idea of people hurting each other. Also, if the war ends, maybe my family could live together again.

Dogs scare me more than anything else. Also little bugs, because they bite. The thing that makes me the most happy is when I play on Play Station. But I have only one wish. That is go to back to America and live with my father. I don't know what I'd do there, but I'd be with him, and it's a better place than here.

# Danielle and Gili, 8

**Even very young children feel the impact of the war, on both sides of the conflict. A study prepared by the University of Tel Aviv's School of Social Work says all Palestinian and Israeli children show some signs of mental and emotional distress. Many have full-blown post traumatic stress disorder. The emotional suffering of these children is bad enough to affect how they manage their daily lives.**

**The distress is greater the closer the child is to the actual fighting, but it still exists even for those whose economic and national status provide a cushion from the battlefield. Most Israeli children know of someone killed or hurt in a bombing or a battle. All are faced with daily searches by armed guards, even if they go to the market with their parents to buy groceries for supper.**

**Friends Danielle and Gili are sitting in McDonald's on a pretty downtown street in West Jerusalem. They are having a meal with their mothers and a very noisy two-year-old brother. The McDonald's looks the same as McDonald's restaurants everywhere, with the exception of the guards at the door, who search everyone's bags as they come in.**

## Danielle

I celebrated my birthday the other day. I had a party with my family, and I had another party with my friends. At the party with my friends, we had pizza, which is my favorite food. We played a lot of games, like statues. Statues is when you move around to music, and when the music stops, you have to freeze in that position. It's hard to do without laughing. It's fun.

I'm in grade three. I have a brother who is going to be four soon, and two stepsisters who are bigger than me. My mom brought me to McDonald's today as a treat.

Jerusalem is a good city to live in. There are a lot of nice places to see, like parks and museums. We go to places on school trips, and sometimes I go with my family. The place I like to go to the best is the zoo. They called it the Biblical Zoo, because there's a Noah's Ark there – not the real one, just a pretend one. I think I like the giraffes best, but I change my mind on that.

Another place I like to be in is South Africa. I have an uncle who lives there, and he has kids who are my cousins. We go there almost every year. Usually we go for Hanukkah, but this year we're going for Passover instead. My cousins and I will set a tent up in the back yard and sleep out there, away from the grown-ups. We always have a midnight feast, too, with lots of sweets, although we can't always stay awake as long as midnight.

I know there is a war going on, but I don't know why. I would rather there was peace. I hear about bombs on television, about bombs going off in shops and on buses, and it makes me afraid. My parents get worried looks on their faces when they read the newspaper or listen to the radio.

I don't know why the Palestinians are so angry with us. We're nice people. I don't know any Palestinians. If I could meet a Palestinian girl my age, we could play together. That way she could see that I'm nice and friendly and she won't want to blow me up.

Bombs scare me more than anything else. I don't know when they will explode. They could explode when I'm shopping for shoes or riding on a bus. I wouldn't have to be doing anything wrong for a bomb to get me.

A bomb won't get me in McDonald's, though. There are guards at the door, and they search everyone on their way in. They searched me and looked through my backpack.

Most buildings have guards who search. You have to let

them, or they will think you are going to blow something up, and be mad at you.

Sometimes if I have candy or something I'm not supposed to have in my bag, I don't want the guard to see it, but they don't really care about that sort of thing. They just want to see if there's a bomb in my bag.

I want to be many things when I grow up. I want to be an artist. I want to dance. And I want to be very, very old, even older than my parents.

My three wishes? I have four: to have more wishes, to be a queen, to get whatever I want when I want it, and to see some TV stars for real.

## Gili

I am in grade three. My best subject is art. I love to draw, especially horses. I like to paint pictures, too. I don't have any brothers or sisters.

I was born in the Ukraine, but I was adopted when I was two months old and brought to Israel. I don't know anything about the Ukraine, except that it gets very cold there. There's special Ukrainian food, too, but it doesn't really have anything to do with me. I'm Israeli, and that's what I feel like.

Horses are my favorite thing. I ride horses at a farm near Jerusalem. I wish I could do that every day, because I would rather ride horses and be around horses more than anything else. I want to have my own horse and be a veterinarian or a professional rider when I grow up, so I can be around horses as much as I want to. And my very, very special dream is to one day visit all the horse farms in the world.

I hear a lot about the war. I'm eight, which is not too young to know about war and bombs.

We have guards at our school to keep the Palestinians from blowing us up. One of the guards there was killed by a bomb.

He wasn't killed at our school, but somewhere else. I was very sad when I heard about it. I was afraid, too. Guards are supposed to protect us, but he couldn't protect himself. If a bomb can kill a guard, it can also kill me or my family.

There is always a lot of talk about war. I have my own gas mask. All the kids at my school have one. This way, we can still breathe if someone drops gas on us. There should be gas masks for horses, too.

I don't like to think about the war. I like to think about horses. I don't want to hurt anybody, and I don't want anybody to hurt me. I just want to ride horses.

Sometimes a long time can go by when I can forget about the war. I have a very nice life, and I can laugh and be with my friends, and then it's like there is no war. Then something happens, like a bus blowing up, and I have to think about it again.

I don't have a horse of my own. I keep asking my mother if I could keep one in my bedroom, and she always says no! I do have a little dog, though, named Blackie. The thing that makes me happiest, other than horses, is playing with Blackie. The thing that I am most afraid of is that I'll fall off a horse.

I don't know if there are Palestinian girls who love horses as much as I do. I don't know any Palestinian girls.

I think about God sometimes. I know God exists. I can feel it, and I know everything will be all right.

# Mona and Mahmood, 11

Living in Palestine and Israel means living with borders. There are borders that divide Israeli land from Palestinian land. There are borders dividing the Israeli settlements from the Palestinian territory they occupy. And there are borders, roadblocks and checkpoints dividing cities and neighborhoods from each other. Roadblocks are roads that have had rubble pushed onto them by the Israeli military so that cars can no longer drive down them. Checkpoints are places where soldiers check the identity papers of everyone passing through.

To reach the settlements, the Israelis have built a series of roads through Palestinian territory. Only Israelis can drive on these roads. Palestinians are not allowed even to cross them without special permits. The roads and roadblocks have divided Palestinian territory in the West Bank into more than twenty separate sections. To get from one place to another, Palestinians must pass through Israeli military checkpoints.

Rawdat-El-Zahur means Garden of Flowers. It is the name of a school in East Jerusalem, which is in Palestinian territory. It is a school for both Christian and Muslim children, run by a Palestinian women's organization. They would like to have Jewish students there as well, and hope this will one day be possible. The school uses music and theater to educate children about peace and human rights. The children, in turn, educate others through their performances.

The school used to hold regular field trips and picnics, but these have not been possible for the past few years, because the children are not able to cross the checkpoints. Classes sometimes do without teachers, when the teachers are stopped by the checkpoints as well.

The walls of the school are covered with the students' colorful artwork. Many of the paintings show things they would like to be able to do, like go on picnics and play in parks. Others show the tanks and soldiers they see around their homes.

Mona and Mahmood are students in this school.

## Mona

I am a Palestinian. That's what I am. How could I be anything else? I wouldn't want to be from anywhere other than Palestine, but I wish life here were easier. I know life is easier for kids in other places, and I wish it were easier for us, just for a little while. I get tired of all the troubles. There never seems to be an end to them.

I live in between Jerusalem and Ramallah, in Palestinian territory. I have three brothers and sisters. I am in the middle. They bother me sometimes, and sometimes I bother them, but that's the way it is with brothers and sisters. The older ones try to tell me what to do, and the younger ones never do what

A roadblock of wrecked cars in Ramallah.

I tell them. When the curfew is gone, and we can go outside and get away from each other, then we can get along. When there is a curfew and we are all locked inside, we have nothing to do but fight.

My favorite thing to do is to paint and draw. I want to learn to paint beautiful things. If all I had to do every day was paint pictures, I would be very happy, and nothing would make me angry. I would like to be a famous artist when I grow up, and have my paintings hang in art galleries all over the world. I would be so famous the Israelis would have to let me cross the checkpoints to visit my paintings.

Where I live is not far from this school, but I have to leave my house at five-thirty in the morning to get through the checkpoint in time to get to school. Even then, I am often late. I don't like getting out of bed when it is still dark, especially in the winter. I know I'll have to spend a long time waiting at the checkpoints, and it makes me want to stay in bed and not bother to go to school. Even if I do good in school, the Israelis will not let us succeed. They like us to feel ashamed of ourselves.

If I get to the checkpoint any later in the morning, I have to wait in an even longer line-up, as there are lots of Palestinians trying to get through to go to their jobs. There are not enough jobs in Palestine, so they have to go to Israel to work. Sometimes the line moves faster than at other times. Sometimes the soldiers make us wait and wait while they have their coffee and cigarettes. There is nothing to do at the checkpoint, except stand and wait until they are ready to let us through.

There isn't even a bathroom. I don't drink anything before I leave home, in case I get stuck at the checkpoint and have to go to the bathroom. That's happened to me before. It's awful. Even without that, my feet get sore from standing and I get bored, bored, bored. It's especially awful when the line isn't

At a checkpoint.

moving, and nobody comes to tell us why it isn't moving, or when we might get through. The soldiers don't care that we are people. They think we are goats who don't mind standing around. But even goats get grass to chew. We get nothing.

If there's been a bombing somewhere, the lines move very slowly. The soldiers search everybody, even children, and check our papers, search our bags and ask us too many questions. They look at me and ask me my name and where I am going. I answer them, and they look at me as if I am lying, then they ask me again. Sometimes I start to worry that maybe I am lying, even though I'm not. Even after all those questions, they sometimes still say no.

I just want to go to school. I don't want to blow anything up. The soldiers don't see me as a child. They see me as an enemy. I don't like them, but I'm not their enemy. I just want to go to school.

Sometimes the soldiers don't bother me too much because I get to the checkpoint so early. The nighttime soldiers just want to go home, and the daytime soldiers aren't awake enough yet to be really mean. Just the same, I don't like having to tell them who I am and where I'm going every day. They don't have to tell me anything. Why should I tell them?

The checkpoints change places all the time. Sometimes when we go to school, we see a checkpoint that wasn't there the night before. They have big cement blocks that they put up in rows, and fences, and guardhouses full of sandbags in case they get bombed. All the soldiers have guns. I often see tanks, too.

There's nothing to do in the line-up. We could talk, but there's not much to say besides complaining. That gets boring, because it doesn't make the line move any faster. We stand and wait, or we sit in the dirt and wait. When it rains, we get wet.

My father works as a taxi driver. He can only drive people up to the checkpoint, then they have to walk across and find another taxi on the other side. When there is a curfew on, he can't drive at all, and I can't come to school. When there are a lot of curfews, or they go on for a long time, my father can't work. Then my parents argue about money, because there isn't much of it in the house.

Soldiers scare me more than anything else. Guns and soldiers. You don't have to be a bad person to get shot by them. Mostly, it is good people who get shot. You should have to do something bad to get shot, but here, everybody gets shot.

The fighting is between the innocent Palestinians, who have nothing, and the Israelis, who have everything. I wish all the Israelis would leave my country. I don't know any Israeli children, and I don't want to, because they have the same beliefs as their parents. They believe that I am not as good as they are. They are not the same as me. I don't know exactly how they are different from me, but they are.

It is hard to have a normal life because we are always holding our breath to see who will be shot next, who will be arrested next, when the next curfew will be. I can never plan to do anything with my friends because the Israelis always ruin our plans. I can't even plan to go over to my friend's house after school, because the soldiers might make it impossible for us to do that.

I want the soldiers to go away and stop bothering us, and let us live our lives.

When there is peace, we will be very happy, and we will be able to go anywhere we want to in our land, without having to cross a checkpoint or explain ourselves to a foreign soldier. I don't know how or when this peace will come. I can't really imagine it.

A volunteer who came here from Canada to help teach us told me there are no checkpoints in Canada. People who live there can start to go somewhere, and they can just go and go and go, without soldiers stopping them and asking them a lot of questions, and keeping them from going where they want to. That must be very nice. I would like to be able to do that one day, just go and go and go and go.

## Mahmood

I live in Beit Hanina, which is only 5 kilometers (3 miles) from my school. To get here, I have to leave my house at six-thirty in the morning. I am lucky if I get to school by a quarter to nine. Most of that time, I am waiting in line to get through the checkpoints.

Last Wednesday, the day before Eid, I saw a mother with a sick baby. She was just ahead of us in the line. We waited for more than two hours, while the line didn't move. Then she left the line to talk with the soldiers. She asked them to let her through because of her baby needing to see a doctor. The soldiers said no and sent her to the back of the line. They wouldn't let us give her her old place in line back. The soldiers don't even care about a sick baby.

I felt kind of ashamed of myself that day. I wish I had stood up to the soldiers and let that woman into the line in front of me. Instead I had to stand with the others and watch her carry her baby to the end of the line. I don't like feeling ashamed. It makes me feel small. I would rather do things that make me feel big, and proud of myself.

There are lots of soldiers where I live. When the soldiers see crowds of Palestinians, they shoot their guns and they drop gas on people. The gas makes my throat hurt and my eyes water up like I'm crying. The gas makes me vomit. When they drop gas on us, I can see a lot of people throwing up. The gas smells bad, too. It doesn't matter if I am outside or inside, because the gas comes into the house. You can't keep it out. It is like air.

They drop gas on us so they can watch us cough and throw up. The soldiers all have gas masks, and they all laugh at us when we're throwing up.

I had a doctor's appointment one day, and when it was over, I had to stay in the doctor's office. The doctor said it wasn't safe for me to go outside. There was a lot of shooting going on in the streets. I looked out of the window and saw many soldiers running by. The doctor told me to get away from the window, or I could get shot, too. I did what he told me to do. I wanted to see what was going on, but I didn't want to get shot.

The shooting always happens all of a sudden. You don't know when it's going to happen, so you can't be ready for it. You have to just be ready all the time. You can never think it's over. You can never relax.

Soldiers scare me more than anything else. That's because they could shoot me whenever they want to, whether I am doing something wrong or not. They don't need a reason. I don't know if they have to wait until someone gives them an order to shoot, or if they can just shoot whenever they feel like it. I think it's whenever they feel like it.

When I play with my friends, we play Israelis and Palestinians, and we pretend to shoot each other. Everyone wants to be Palestinians, of course, but we trade off, to make it fair. We have toy machine guns and rifles, but we also make our own guns out of sticks and things, so that there are enough guns to go around. We play around the ruins of buildings that have been bombed, jumping out at each other. In our game, the Palestinians always win.

I play games where we shoot the Israelis, but the guns aren't real, and no one really gets hurt. I wouldn't want to hurt anybody for real. Also, we Palestinians are forbidden by the Israelis to have guns. They want to keep all the guns for themselves.

I don't know any Israeli children. I don't want to know any. They hate me, and I hate them.

# Gul, 12

There is conscription in Israel, which means that all young men must serve in the military when they turn eighteen or so. There are a few exceptions to this. Ultra-orthodox Jews and Israeli Arabs do not have to serve.

Young women are encouraged to join the army, too. Those who choose to do so serve alongside the men, doing most of the same jobs that the men do.

Young men who refuse to go into the military may be declared mentally unfit, a label that follows them throughout their lives. They could also be sent to jail.

Some young men do not support what their government is doing in the Palestinian territories. They refuse to go into the army as a protest or, if they are already in the military, they refuse to serve in the territories. There are more than 450 of these protestors, or refuseniks, as they are called. Many have been put in jail for taking such a stand.

Gul lives in a tree-lined residential neighborhood in West Jerusalem. Both of his parents are professionals. Their apartment is full of books and plants. Although he is a few years from conscription age, the choices he will face are very much on his mind.

I am in grade seven. My favorite subject is English.

I live with my mother, father and older brother in an apartment on the top floor of a small apartment building. It's a very nice area, with lots of trees along the streets. The Jews who came here many years ago are the ones who planted the trees, and now they are big and make the street very shady.

I will soon be thirteen, and will, of course, have my bar mitzvah. There will be a special ceremony in the synagogue. I will have to read from the Torah and make a speech. It will

A boy reads the Torah at the Western Wall in Jerusalem.

mean that I have become a man under Jewish law. I haven't started thinking about it yet. I don't have to start studying for it until next week. Then I will start to think about it. I'll have two parties after the ceremony. One will be with my family, and one with my friends.

I like living in Jerusalem. It's the center of everything in Israel. There's a lot to do here, like movies, sports, lots of things.

We live in the new part of the city. There's also the Old City, which is where all the history happened. It's thousands of years old. We go there on school trips. I don't go there on my own. There is enough to do in the new city without going there, but I like seeing it from a distance. When the sun is shining on the walls, it looks very beautiful, like out of a book, only better.

I don't like it that I will have to join the army in a few years, but I don't have a choice. Maybe by then I'll feel differently, but I don't think so. I've never played soldiers or games like that. Some kids like that sort of thing, but I don't. I prefer basketball.

Sometimes the army goes into Palestinian cities like Hebron or Bethlehem. They take Palestinians out of their homes, then bulldoze the homes so there is nothing left. They do that in case there's a bomb inside the house. The soldiers might have to be rough to get the Palestinians out of their house, because they won't want to leave. It's their home, and they want to stay there.

My mother doesn't want me being rough and mean to people when I'm a soldier. She says she's brought us up to be kind to people. She thinks going into the army will change the kind of person I am. I don't see how that can happen. I am who I am. How can anything change that?

It's always there, the army, when I think of the future. All boys have to go into the army. It's the law.

I have an older sister, Ori. She's eighteen now and decided to do National Community Service instead of going into the army. She's living in Tel Aviv, in a house with other girls. She does some sort of work with children. She thinks the occupation is bad, and doesn't want to be part of it. She says if she went into the army she'd have to kill people if she was ordered to, and she doesn't want to do that.

It's easier for her to not go into the army because she's a girl, but I have heard a lot of people arguing with her about it.

They think it's everyone's duty to defend Israel. So even though she's contributing to the country through National Service, people still think she is shirking.

Boys don't have that choice. Boys have to join the army, unless they are very religious. Then they don't have to.

Sometimes I think it could be fun to be in the army. I look at all the soldiers in the streets, and they can do so many things, like drive tanks and work radios, and they look strong and smart.

They came to my class at school to show us how to wear our gas masks. We all have our own gas mask, in case the Palestinians or the Iraqis drop poison gas on us. The soldiers explained everything and they were really confident. I would like to be like that.

I try to imagine myself being one of them, doing things like searching Palestinian homes and driving a tank into their cities. Maybe by the time I have to join the army, there will be peace, and I won't have to do those things.

The soldiers do those things because of the bombs. The Palestinians put bombs on buses and in restaurants. I know someone who was almost killed by a bomb. He was in the market, and got on a bus to go home. The bus started, and the bomb went off. He had bruises, but he was not killed. Other people were killed that day, but I don't know how many.

Things were quiet here for awhile. When the violence started up again, my parents didn't want me to go downtown, in case there was a bomb. Sometimes we'd drive through there, and it would be very quiet because everyone was scared and was staying home. It's busy there now, but there is security everywhere. The soldiers stop everyone and search their bags and things. My friends and I are still nervous on buses.

Sometimes there are bombs in cars parked along the sides of the street. They blow up and kill the people walking by. When I'm outside I think about that. Every car I walk beside is one that could blow up and kill me. It's pretty scary, so I try not to think about it.

All I know about this war is that it's about this country, this land. The Palestinians want it, and we want it, so we're fighting over it. I don't know how it will end, or if it ever will.

I met some Palestinians once, in Abu Gosh, a village near Jerusalem. They were pretty nice kids, no different from me. I don't know any Palestinians now, though. They can't come here, and it's too dangerous for us to go there.

It's dangerous for Jews in a lot of places. The Palestinians are not the only people in the world who hate Jews. My mother has a friend in Montreal, in Canada, who has told her stories about people hating Jews there. People have always hated Jews everywhere, not just Germans, and not just Palestinians.

# Yanal, 14

Allowed almost no freedom of movement, many young Palestinians give up hope of ever being able to accomplish something positive with their lives. Some have been granted scholarships to universities in Jordan and elsewhere, but they are refused permission to leave. Palestinians from the territories are also not allowed to fly out of Ben Gurian  Airport in Tel Aviv. If the school they have been accepted to is in another Palestinian town, they may have to give up that chance because of being unable to cross the roadblocks.

According to UNICEF, more than 60 percent of Palestinians are under eighteen. There are almost a million Palestinians of school age. Palestinian literacy rates are among the highest in the region, and Palestinian girls were the first in the Arab world to reach educational parity with their brothers.

The occupation has disrupted their education, as Palestinian schools are often shut down during curfews. Some schools have been turned into detention centers by the Israeli military. Others have been partially damaged or totally destroyed in the war. The roadblocks and checkpoints have prevented more than 200,000 children and more than 9,000 teachers from reaching their regular schools. In some places, makeshift schools have been set up in mosques, basements and alleyways.

The destruction of the Palestinian economy due to the war has made it difficult for many parents to afford the things their children need for school. UNICEF has a campaign to supply the most desperate children with school uniforms, book bags and supplies.

Even those able to complete school have little hope of finding a job. Among Palestinians the unemployment rate is 60 percent on average.

Yanal lives in the West Bank city of Ramallah, a few kilometers north of Jerusalem. It was first inhabited two thousand years ago. French crusaders used it as a base for attacking Jerusalem. Modern settlement there goes back to 1550. Now the Israeli military patrols and controls the area.

Yanal goes to the School of Hope in Ramallah, which has been educating Palestinian children for thirty-five years. They have four hundred students of all ages. Enrollment used to be higher, as students used to come to the school from the villages around Ramallah, but curfews and roadblocks have made it impossible for those children to travel.

I am a Palestinian. I have lived in Ramallah all of my life, except for one year that I spent in Saudi Arabia when I was a baby. I have one brother and one sister. My father is a very learned man. He teaches in a university and has written many books about Palestine. My mother is also an educated woman. She is a school supervisor.

Palestinian children in front of an Israeli tank in Nablus.

Most of the people I know have never left Ramallah. We are very close to Jerusalem, yet we have never been able to go. Half the kids who go to this school are Muslims, and half are Christians. Now we are celebrating both Advent for the Christians, and Ramadan for the Muslims. There are many holy places in Jerusalem for both of us, yet we cannot go to see them.

Being religious, whether you are Muslim or Christian or Jewish, or whatever you are, means that you should help people, and make the world better, and not just think of yourself. We have these things in common, at least in our religions.

I want to be a professional singer. I want that with every part of me. My friend tells me, "You are just a Palestinian. No one will want to buy your CDs. No one will want to hear your songs."

Palestinian children walk through the rubble of a destroyed metal shop in Gaza City.

I don't agree with my friend. I will make people want to listen.

People believe what they see on the news, and since the Israelis control the news, people think all Palestinians are bad. They don't think we are regular human beings.

Israeli kids get hatred put inside them by their parents and their government. They don't know anything real about us. They think Palestinians don't know anything about books or culture. They think we are animals who don't know how to read or do anything that takes brains. Because they don't know us, they want to kill us. The Israeli people need to fight back at the lies they get told about us.

Living under occupation is very difficult. There are always soldiers around to tell us that we are worthless criminals, even worse than criminals. I feel good about myself because I am a Palestinian and a good person, but not everyone feels this way about themselves. The Israelis want us to hate ourselves. Then we won't bother to resist them. If we think we are nothing, then it won't matter if we are under occupation. We won't think we deserve anything better.

My school has just reopened after three days of curfew. Being under curfew means everything shuts down, and everyone has to stay inside or get shot.

Israeli soldiers occupied our school last spring. We were under curfew when they came, so the school was empty, but they barged in anyway. They made holes in the doors, broke windows and furniture, they smashed everything. They wrote rude things on the blackboards. They even peed on the floors. And they call *us* animals.

We all worked together to clean it up. It took us three days. It made me angry, but it made me feel strong, too, that we can fix whatever the Israelis try to do to us.

My mother inspects schools. There are a lot of strong

Palestinian women, and my mother is one of them. She goes around to schools and makes sure they have everything they need. She travels all over the area, to Bethlehem and to Nablus. She can't go all the time. She often gets turned back at the checkpoints. If she's not turned back, they make her sit and wait. Once she was trying to get home, and they made her wait for five hours. It was late, and she wanted to get home. They told her to sleep on the ground until they were ready to let her cross. One time they told her to get down on her hands and knees and eat grass, then they would let her cross. She didn't do it. She won't let them bully her.

It is very hard for women at the checkpoints. They have no place to go when, you know, they have to go. Men can go by the side of the road if we have to, but women can't.

Some of the checkpoints have special cement buildings. If the soldiers want to, they take someone into the building and make them take off their clothes. They say this is to search for bombs, but no one with a bomb would be stupid enough to try to take it through a checkpoint. I think they do it just to humiliate us. They beat people in those buildings, too, because no one can see them do it. My mother sometimes sees Israeli women standing at the checkpoints with cameras, to take pictures of the soldiers if they are not behaving properly. Not all Israelis are our enemy.

My mother has spent a lot of time in line-ups at checkpoints. She has heard lots of stories, of women having their babies right there at the border, and people being very, very ill, and not being able to cross over to go to the doctor.

Sometimes Ramallah is open only for one hour a day. We never know when the curfew will be lifted, or for how long, so we always have to be ready to go out and shop for food or send messages, or do other things we need to do. A woman my parents knew washed her family's clothes and put them out in the sun to dry on her balcony when the curfew was lifted. Then the curfew started again, but the clothes were still wet. She went out onto her balcony to get them when they were dry, but it was after curfew. One of the soldiers saw her and shot her and killed her.

When I hear things like that, I cry.

Some Israelis want peace. When someone in their family dies because of the war, they feel sad, just like we feel when someone in a Palestinian family dies. In that way, we are the same.

My mother has been shot at many times by the soldiers as she goes from school to school. She was in a library once. She had just left it when the Israelis bombed it, and it exploded behind her. Why would they blow up a library? It makes no sense. I think the Israelis just like to bomb, and they don't care what the bomb blows up.

The Israelis change their minds all the time about curfews. It makes me angry, because I can't plan anything, like when to see my friends, when to go to the shops. It makes no sense, what they do. If something happens in Jenin, they close Ramallah. They say it's for security, but I think they just like to punish us.

I was in a movie theater with my friends once. In the middle of the movie, the Israelis announced a curfew. We were ordered back into our homes and didn't get to see the rest of the film. It was an American film called "Save the Last Dance," with Julia Stiles. It was about two very different people who came together through dance and music. I liked it very much, and would like to know how it ends.

Music is everything to me. It helps me when I'm angry, and it makes me feel better when I am sad. When I'm happy, music makes me even happier.

In many ways, I can understand the suicide bombers. When you've lost everyone, when you have no one left to rely on, and no hope that things will get better, why stay alive? I heard about a five-year-old boy. He was in school, and he came home to find his family all dead and his house destroyed. What can he do? He will be sad for the rest of his life. I am glad every day that my parents are still alive.

Setting off bombs in shopping centers, though, is not a good idea. It makes the Palestinians look bad. We should be terrorizing the Israeli soldiers, not the Israeli people. Besides, the bombs could hurt us, too.

I wish the fighting would end, so that we can just make music and have fun and not hate each other. Maybe we could even make music with the Israelis one day.

# Merav, 13

Settlements are Israeli communities that have been built on Palestinian land occupied by the Israeli army after the 1967 war. They were begun by people who wanted to claim that land for Israel even though under international law, the land belongs to the Palestinians. People who live in these settlements receive tax breaks and help from the  government with housing and school fees. The settlements are guarded by the army and by the settlers themselves, many of whom carry weapons for protection.

There are now more than two hundred settlements in the West Bank, Gaza and Greater Jerusalem. Many of these settlements began as small collections of trailers and makeshift homes, but they have been built up by the government and the people who live there, and now look like thriving towns with modern houses, schools, parks and shops. More than 400,000 Israelis now live in the settlements.

Bypass roads connect the settlements to each other and, often, to Jerusalem and other major cities. These are roads

An Israeli settlement.

that only Israelis can drive on. They are often surrounded by high walls, which provide some protection from rock throwers and snipers. Since the roads, like the settlements, are in Palestinian territory, there is much anger among the Palestinians about their construction.

The settlers also place further stress on water supplies in the area, with the bulk of the available water being diverted to the settlements. One Israeli consumes as much water as four Palestinians.

There is a difference in lifestyle as well. With the Palestinians confined to small enclosed areas and most unable to cross the checkpoints, the Palestinian economy has suffered. Since Israelis are freer to come and go, their economy is stronger. Palestinians living in poverty can look out their windows and see prosperous settlements with swimming pools and other amenities. This makes them resent the Israelis even more. Sometimes the settlements are attacked, and settlers are killed. Sometimes some of these settlers attack the Palestinians.

A new security wall is being built around the West Bank. In some places it will be a cement wall that is 8 meters (25 feet) high. In other places it will be an electrified fence. This wall will stretch for 650 kilometers (400 miles), snaking around the settlements and further dividing Palestinian territory into small pockets of land that the Palestinians cannot leave freely. The fence will have guard towers every 300 meters (900 feet), a deep trench around it, a security road and motion detectors. Much of the wall is being built on Palestinian land. Olive groves, citrus orchards and farm land have been bulldozed to make space for it.

Many Israelis believe this wall is necessary to protect them from the Palestinians. Others believe it makes the situation worse. People in Israel do not agree about the settlements, either. Some believe they only escalate the war, and

The wall surrounding the city of Qalqiyah.

there are many calls for the settlements to be dismantled. A lot of soldiers are required to protect the settlers, and the soldiers' presence in Palestinian territory makes the Palestinians fight back, which prompts the soldiers to fight the Palestinians, and on and on it goes.

There are others in Israel who see the settlements as being important for Israel's security. They see the settlers as brave pioneers who have made tremendous sacrifices to live and raise their children in the middle of an unfriendly environment.

Merav lives in a settlement near Efrat.

Efrat is between Jerusalem and Hebron. It's a nice town with shopping centers, pizza places, playgrounds, parks – all the normal things. It's a very beautiful place to live, too, because it is in the Judean Hills. I like living there very much. People have come to live there from many other places, like the United States, Canada, England, Russia and South Africa.

I came to Hebron today with my family to take part in a Hanukkah party. Hanukkah is a very happy holiday. It celebrates a time when, long ago, the Greeks took over a Jewish temple. They destroyed all the special oil for the lamps. When the Jews took back the temple, they found just one bottle of oil that hadn't been ruined. It was only enough oil to keep the lamps burning for one day but, by a miracle, it kept them burning for eight days! So we celebrate the miracle by lighting the menorah candles, eating holiday food like fried latkes, and having parties and getting presents.

At night we put the lit menorahs in doorways and windows. The lights look very beautiful. They are supposed to remind us that God is always with us, even when we are afraid and think we are alone. God means that I have to try to be the very best person I can be. I have to act to a very high standard.

There are a lot of people here today from around Jerusalem. They came on buses to help us celebrate Hanukkah, and because they wanted to show that they support us. By us, they mean settlers. They say we are brave to live in the settlements.

They are giving us kids a party, with a clown and presents to take our minds off the war for a little while. But my mind is not always on the war anyway. I have a lot of other things to think about, like school and friends.

There are a lot of soldiers around my settlement. I feel proud whenever I see them. They are very brave. Their job is to protect me and my family, and I'm glad that they are around. It is very dangerous to live where we live. There are Palestinians all around us, and they are our enemies. We children are always being warned to be careful, to not wander around on our own. There is a high wall being built all around the Palestinian places, which will help to keep us safe.

If you wander around on your own, a Palestinian with a

gun might see you and shoot you. They wait to catch people who are not being careful, who are thinking of other things and not watching out. You can only relax if someone is there to watch out for you.

There have been people killed in Efrat by the Palestinians. Two women were murdered while they were driving to Jerusalem. Others have been killed or shot at. There was a suicide bomber there, too, who tried to kill some medical people.

Most of my friends' families have cars with special glass in the windows to protect them from stones. The Palestinians throw stones at Israeli cars. The buses have bulletproof glass in the windows, so that if we get shot at while we're riding in them, the bullets will just bounce off.

But I don't like to think about the war. There are a lot of other things to think about.

I like spending time with my friends. We belong to the Youth Movement, and do many activities with them, like trips and things. We go to many parts of Israel. Some of the places we go to are very historic. Some are more for fun. We also like to hang out together and talk. Sometimes we discuss world problems. Usually we talk about things that are not so serious, that are just fun.

I had my bat mitzvah last year. It's a ceremony for girls that means we are no longer children. The ceremony took place in our synagogue. This means that I now have more responsibility, like an adult instead of a child. It means I am ready to be more involved in the world.

I don't plan on joining the army when I'm older. Lots of girls do, and I am not against the army, but I'll do National Voluntary Service instead, maybe in a hospital.

I don't know any Palestinian children. They are all around the outside of my settlement, but I don't know any of them. I have no reason to meet them. They are dangerous and will shoot me if they get the chance. The Israeli army keeps them away from us.

My friends and family and I live in the middle of the war. It is scary, being surrounded by people who want to kill us, but we have to have hope.

# Maryam, 11

**Maryam lives in Bethany, not far from Jerusalem. Her grand-mother lives and works in East Jerusalem. Maryam does not have the papers that give her permission to**  **cross the checkpoints between Bethany and Jerusalem, and her grandmother cannot cross the checkpoints, either. The only way they can see each other is if they avoid the checkpoints and roads and walk across the desert hills from one city to the other. Maryam usually makes the journey with her aunt, who also does not have the right papers. They do this at great risk, and would likely be arrested if they were caught by the Israeli army.**

I live in a town outside of Jerusalem called Bethany. I'm not supposed to be here in Jerusalem. I don't have the right papers, but my Aunt Talal and I walked across the hills, away from the checkpoints. My aunt is eighteen and very brave. We snuck past the soldiers. It was fun, but also scary, because it is very dangerous. If we were caught, the soldiers would arrest us. They would treat us badly, but they will have to catch us first! I don't like soldiers.

We walked here today so I could visit my grandmother. She manages a youth hostel in Jerusalem. People come here to stay from all over the world. Sometimes they sit and talk with me and share their snacks with me. I like that. I would like to go to other places, too.

Bethany is a beautiful old city. It is in Palestinian territory. It is full of shops, churches and mosques. The streets are wide, and there are many buildings.

There are many, many Israeli soldiers in my city. They walk on the sidewalks and drive in the streets, in jeeps and trucks and tanks. They try to make us believe it is their city and not ours. It is very bad. We cannot be at home in our own home. They treat it like it is their home.

I even see a lot of soldiers around my school. They are always there, all the time. They watch me whenever I go out with my friends or my teachers. I can feel them watching me, and I wish they would look in another direction. I'm not doing anything wrong, and I don't like to be watched. They stop me in the streets and ask me questions. They stare at me and say nasty, rude things to me and my friends. They say things to my aunt that are disrespectful, things that men should not say to women. I don't like talking to them, but I can't avoid them. If they ask me a question and I refuse to answer, they might shoot me.

I see the bad things they do, and I hear about more bad things on television. They fly their helicopters over my city and shoot their guns at people. They want us to be ashamed of being Palestinian, but I'm not ashamed. I'm proud of it.

I used to cry when I saw the soldiers, but I don't do that anymore. They still scare me, but I don't like to let them see that. I'm more angry than I am afraid, I think. I would like to kill the soldiers, but I can't, because I have no weapons.

One of my cousins is in an Israeli prison. He is twenty years old. He has been in prison for eight months and has to be in there for two years more. He was in college when he was arrested. He wants to be an accountant, which I don't want to be. He didn't do anything wrong, but the Israelis arrested him anyway. He was part of a Palestinian organization, and the Israelis didn't like that. His mother has been able to visit him in jail. I'm glad about that. It would be awful to be in jail and have no one visit you.

I sleep in the school I go to. I live there. My mother died when I was five. She was killed in a car accident. She was thirty-nine. My aunt is kind to me, and so is my grandmother, but I still miss my mother. I miss her all the time. She used to sing to me.

There are other girls at my school who have lost their mothers, or even both parents. We all sleep in the same room. I have a best friend there who is very kind to me. I try to be kind to her, too.

My favorite story is *Beauty and the Beast*. I like the Beauty person the best. I also like to play games on the computer, like solitaire.

Most days at school are the same. We get up at seven and do chores, like cleaning the bedroom and sweeping the hallways. Then we eat breakfast, then we go to school. Religion is my favorite subject because it's easy, and it teaches me many new things about what kind of person to be.

My school isn't a bad place, although I get lonely. The worst thing is this tomato and vegetable dish they make us eat

Soldiers in the Palestinian part of Hebron, with the town under curfew.

sometimes. I hate that. The thing I like to eat the most is mak-louba, which is chicken and rice, but we don't have that very often.

When there is a curfew, everything shuts down. All the shops have to close, and everyone has to stay home. You can't even look out the window or the soldiers will shoot at you. It is like the whole city is in jail, only their jail is their homes. The soldiers never tell us why they are making us stay inside. They just tell us to go inside and stay there.

My aunt calls the time we have to stay inside wasted time.

It's not wasted so much for me, since I live in the same place where I go to school. Some of the children in my school live at their homes, and they have to stay there when there is a curfew on. They get to miss school. Many of the teachers can't come when there is a curfew, so it is a bit like a holiday for us. It gets boring, though. It would be more of a holiday if we could go outside and do things.

The teachers are very strict at my school. When there is a curfew and they can't leave, they get into bad moods. I get punished a lot for being noisy. They hit me on the hand with their hand, and make me stand in the corner. I want to be a doctor when I grow up, but first I have to finish school. That seems like a very long time to go.

My aunt says that we shouldn't let boys tell us we can't do things just because we're girls. She says that Palestinian girls and women are strong and brave, and we can fight the Israelis just as well as the boys can. I think she's right. She's a strong woman, and I'm going to be just like her.

There are women martyrs now who do the suicide bomb-ings. They are very brave. It must be very difficult for their families.

I have only one wish. I would like to go to heaven. Maybe in heaven there is happiness, after we die. Maybe then.

## Elisheva, 18

Most Israelis know someone who has been touched directly by the violence, either by being wounded themselves, or knowing someone who has been wounded or killed. Memorials to those who have been killed in the war are everywhere, from park benches named in memory of a child who used to love the park, to trees planted in memory of someone's father.  Elisheva is still grieving the loss of her two friends who were killed recently by a Palestinian. She helps other kids who are also in her position through Kids for Kids, an organization that supports those who have experienced violence from the war.

I live in a settlement north of Jerusalem. I have two older brothers and one older sister. One of my brothers is married and has two children. My favorite book is *Anne of Green Gables*. My favorite singer is Celine Dion, and my favorite movie is "The Horse Whisperer."

My father is a psychologist. He specializes in terror, trauma and family problems. He has lots of chances to practice his specialty in Israel these days. There are a lot of people who have trauma problems, from all the bombings that are going on.

I am in grade twelve. I like everything in school. I attend a religious school, so in addition to regular subjects, I study a lot of books about the Bible. It brings back good memories of when I first heard those stories when I was a child. Living in Israel is wonderful, because this is the place where most of those stories really happened.

When I finish high school, I will do National Service for two years. Many religious girls do that instead of going into the army. I'd like to volunteer with children who have emotional problems or problems in school, maybe as a tutor, or at a recreation center. You know, get them involved in activities to keep their spirits up.

I've traveled a lot in Israel. We go on two or three school trips a year, sometimes more. We study something in history class and go to see the place where it happened.

It is very hard living in Israel in the current situation. There is a lot of fear. Two of my good friends and one of my teachers were killed by Palestinian bombs, but because I am religious, and I believe that God is with us, I will be strong. God gives me strength and gives my life meaning. I don't know how non-religious people manage.

I'll tell you about one of my friends who died. His name was Avi, and he was seventeen.

He went to school here with me here in the settlement. He

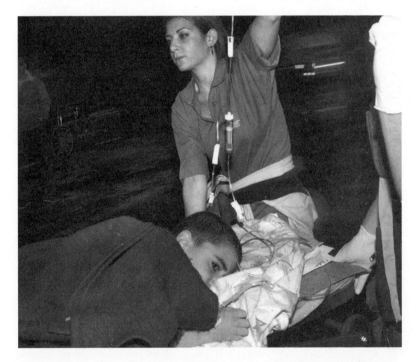

A child is evacuated from a hotel restaurant after a suicide bombing at a hotel in the Israeli town of Netanya.

took a break from studying for a mathematics exam and was playing basketball in the school yard with a few of his friends.

Suddenly, a man appeared with a machine gun. He started shooting, firing all around.

Two boys ran one way, and Avi ran another way. The Arab went after Avi and shot him in the back. He didn't die right away, but it didn't take long.

The gunman went through the school, shooting and yelling before the Israeli army killed him. I don't know what he was shouting.

Shmuel, a friend of Avi's, hid in a bathroom with a few other boys and did not get hurt. When he found out that Avi had been killed, he became very depressed. He felt he should have somehow saved Avi's life and felt bad at being alive when Avi was dead.

Two weeks after Avi died, Shmuel had his seventeenth birthday. Two days after that, Shmuel was killed by a Palestinian bomb as he was waiting for a bus.

I have some very special memories of Avi. He was always playing the guitar. He took it every place. He left the radio on when he went to sleep because he loved music so much. He always had a big smile on his face, and was just a big kid, really. People were always drawn to him, because he liked being alive so much. He liked everyone to be happy.

Shmuel was always able to fix people's problems. He always organized everything and everyone. He was a good listener, too.

There are Palestinians living only half a kilometer (1,500 feet) away from our settlement. We can see their village from our house. We live close to each other, but we live like enemies.

We could have lived like neighbors, and we did for awhile. We went to their weddings and feasts, and they came to ours. I remember when I was little we would go to their parties, and they were always friendly and welcoming. All of that has changed.

Now we don't know who we can trust. In Gaza, Palestinians who have worked for Israelis for years have killed their bosses. Palestinians who used to be friendly now throw stones at our homes and shoot us if they are able to get close enough.

We can't go into the Palestinian villages at all. It is far too risky. Even if we are just going for a walk, we could be shot. The Palestinians don't trust us. They can't come into our settlement, either. Our soldiers won't let them in, and their people will think they are traitors, and kill them.

Whenever we leave the settlement, we have to go in bullet-proof buses. Otherwise we could be shot.

For the situation to get better, we will need to have a very big war. After that everyone will see what the right thing is, and there would be no more need to kill. That would mean peace.

We, the Israelis, have been trying, but how much can we give? After all, this is our land. I wish all the Jews in the world would come to Israel, and that all the Palestinians would leave and go live in some other Arab country.

The death of my friends has changed me a lot. It has strengthened my beliefs. There are people who question the existence of God. I am not one of them. I wish everyone would realize that God is the One, that he guides us and will bring his light to every heart.

It has also made me want to share more time with my friends and family, because you never know what will happen, or when.

Regarding the war with the Palestinians, I've gotten stronger in my belief that we are right. If the Palestinians were right, they wouldn't be so sneaky, so full of tricks.

I feel a lot of anger toward the Palestinians. I can't feel real hate because it's hard for me to find bad things in people, but I still feel anger. When I walk through the Old City of Jerusalem and see the Arabs there, I don't want to see them. I don't want them to be there. They make me angry.

# Hassan, 18

The United Nations Relief and Works Agency (UNRWA) is the UN agency charged with some responsibility for the Palestinian refugees. According to them, Palestinian refugees

are people who lived in Palestine between June 1946 and May 1948 and who lost their homes and means of earning a living in the 1948 war. The descendants of these people are also considered refugees.

There are now about four million Palestinian refugees. One million live in refugee camps. Some of these camps are in Lebanon, Syria and Jordan. Others are in the West Bank and the Gaza Strip.

A Palestinian refugee camp is a piece of land set aside for the use of UNRWA to house Palestinians. The camps look like crowded cities. Cement buildings have replaced what were once canvas tents. Living conditions in the camps are poor, with overcrowding and inadequate roads and sewers.

Whole generations have lived in these camps. They have schools, clinics and other services administered with the aid of UNRWA. Camps are often occupied by the Israeli military and are often the site of street battles between armed Palestinian factions and the Israeli Defence Forces. These battles, and the ongoing tensions, have a profound impact on the children who live there.

Children who have been severely traumatized by war show their pain in many different ways. Some start to wet the bed at night. Others can't sleep, or have nightmares. They are unable to concentrate in school. Some become angry and aggressive and are unable to get along with people even when things are calm. Other children stop talking, a symptom of distress known as elective mutism. Some react by losing some of their physical abilities.

**The Palestinian Rehabilitation Centre in the Ramallah refugee camp is a series of small stone buildings tucked into a courtyard behind an alleyway. It was started by the mothers of hurt children to provide some of the healing their children and others in the community need. When the city is not under curfew, the women who run the place also visit the disabled in their homes and try to encourage them to come out, to be a part of society.**

**Hassan has been in a wheelchair for the past few years. "There is nothing physically wrong with him," his attendant says. "He was frightened so much by the soldiers a few years ago, he became unable to move his legs and one of his arms. He hasn't walked since. There is treatment available for this in other countries, but it is too expensive, and anyway, we can't leave this camp."**

I was born in this camp. This is home to me. I have never lived anywhere else. I have seen pictures of other places. They look quite beautiful. I would like to see them for myself one day, especially places with lots of trees and rivers and lakes. The people in this camp are good people, but the camp is not beautiful. It is all cement and alleys, and there are too often tanks in the streets and soldiers. We hear a lot of gunfire and shooting. I don't like those sounds. I prefer music.

People would make things beautiful here if they could, but no one has any money, so we get used to it being ugly. Anyway, if we made something beautiful, the soldiers would blow it up, or run over it with a tank, and turn it back into garbage. So why would we bother?

A lot of people die in this camp. The Israelis shoot missiles at us. Not long ago, a missile hit a car and killed a woman and her three children. Two other children were killed by a land mine. Lots of people die here.

We hear helicopters at night sometimes, and planes, and

In the refugee camp in Ramallah.

there are sometimes burned-out cars in the streets in the morning that weren't there the night before. People are very nervous. We never know when the soldiers are going to come and bother us.

The soldiers came to this center a little while ago. They broke things and made a mess. It looks good now. People came and cleaned it up. I helped a little bit, but I couldn't help much, because I can't get out of my chair.

The posters on the walls are of martyrs who died trying to free Palestine. They are not cheerful pictures, but they are strong ones.

I went as far as grade six in school. My favorite subject was English. I still like to try to speak English. Maybe I'll visit Canada some day.

I cannot concentrate very well anymore to study, so I did not go past class six.

I come to the center every day, unless there is a curfew.

Someone pushes my wheelchair and brings me here. I do art, and listen to others playing music, and play cards or just talk with people. It is someplace to go.

Eid is coming up soon. Some of the people here are preparing feast dishes to share with Palestinians in the camp who cannot afford to celebrate. There are good cooking smells that come from their work. I hope we are not under curfew for Eid so we can celebrate. I will get some new clothes, and go to the mosque, and visit with the family who are in this camp. The family who are not in this camp, we will not be able to see, because we cannot leave the camp, and they cannot come here.

The thing I enjoy most is hanging out with my friends. We play cards and other games I can play with my hands. The thing that scares me the most is soldiers, because of the weapons they carry. They don't like us. All they want to do is shoot at us and kill us. I wish they would go away.

I would like to be a policeman when I get older. I would be a good policeman. People would trust me, and I would keep them safe.

If I had three wishes, I would walk again, I would play soccer, and I would go to see beautiful places.

# Hakim, 12

Since the beginning of the second Intifada, or Palestinian uprising, thousands of Palestinian civilians have been wounded by the Israeli army or by settlers, or injured during helicopter, tank or fighter-jet attacks on their neighborhoods. Many of these have been children. Children who harass the Israeli army by throwing stones and yelling are likely to be responded to with gunfire and tear gas.

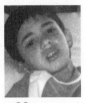

A study done by U.S. AID found that more than 22 percent of Palestinian children suffer from acute or chronic malnutrition, and one-fifth have moderate or severe anemia. Roadblocks, closures, checkpoints and curfews all limit the amount of food that comes into Palestinian territory. And when people are not free to travel to their jobs or farm land, they can't earn enough money to buy proper food when it is available. The study found that more than 40 percent of Palestinian families have sold some of their belongings to buy food. Not having proper food means that children don't grow or develop properly.

Hakim was badly injured by the army. He is a tiny boy, small for his age because of the malnutrition he has suffered. When I meet him, he is lying in bed in a Palestinian hospital, in great pain. His father is with him, and every time a wave of pain flashes across Hakim's face, it is mirrored in his father's face.

I am from the city of Tulkarm, in the West Bank. A week ago the army came in with tanks and guns, looking for someone they didn't like. I knew the man they wanted. His name was Tareq al Zaghal. They found him and killed him. They also killed a boy I knew. His name was Ihab el Zuqla. He was thirteen. They shot him and he died.

I am twelve years old. I am in grade six, but the soldiers make us stay in our homes, so we often have to miss school.

The Israeli soldiers shot up both my legs.

I was in the street with my friends. We were hiding from the soldiers, and when we could, we were throwing rocks at them. The soldiers were angry and they were looking for us. I am a good runner. I wanted to get to another place, and I thought I could run fast enough to get away from the soldiers. I thought I could run faster than the bullets. So I decided to run across the road.

I started running. I ran very fast. In the middle of the road I heard many shots. I stopped feeling anything in my right leg, but I think I kept running. In my head, I remember that I kept running. I didn't know yet that I had been shot.

I heard more bullets. My legs stopped working. I fell down in the street. Some of my friends came and carried me off the road, but they were pushed away by the soldiers.

Palestinian boys throwing rocks at the Israeli army.

I can remember the soldiers standing all around me. I was on the ground staring up at them, and they were all around me, with their guns pointed at me. They wouldn't let my friends come near me. There was a lot of yelling and screaming.

I know the soldiers hated me. I know they wanted to kill me. I don't know why they didn't shoot me then. They had their guns there, and they could have done it because my legs had stopped working and I couldn't run away from them.

There are pins in my legs now, and lots of things wrong with them. The doctors here told me I was shot fifteen times.

It took many more shots than that to kill Tareq. He was a neighbor of mine, the one the Israelis were after. They had to shoot him many times to kill him. The soldiers killed five other Palestinians that day. They like to kill Palestinians.

I cannot leave my bed. My legs are in big casts, and I have to stay on my back all the time. I can't move or go anywhere. If the soldiers come to look for me here, I will not be able to run away from them. My father is here, but he will not be able to protect me.

I am the youngest of three boys in my family. I don't have any sisters. I would like to have a sister. Some of my friends with sisters don't like them, but I would like to know what that is like, having a sister. I am glad my father is staying at the hospital with me so I don't feel lonely. The nurses and doctors here are nice to me, too.

There have always been soldiers in my city. I am not afraid of them. I have my own M16 rifle. It is carved out of a piece of wood. I use it to shoot the soldiers the same way I would if it were a real gun. They do not scare me. The other boys and I, we take care of each other. When someone gets hurt, we all help to carry them off the street, the way they carried me.

I fight the soldiers a lot. It feels good to throw stones at them. They should not be in my town, so I throw stones to make them go away. They do bad things. They arrest Palestinian people, even children, and make them sit with their eyes covered and their hands behind their backs. They blow up people's houses. They make us go hungry. I do not like them.

I have been shot many times by rubber bullets. I have been shot this way in the chest and in the legs. The bullets hurt very much. They leave big bruises on me. First the bruises are green, then they are yellow. I have been shot at with gas, too. It gets in my eyes and makes them hurt and cry.

My legs hurt a lot. All of me hurts today. My legs are in big casts, and I have to just lie here. I can't move them. I can't sit up or walk or do anything.

I don't know any Israelis. I don't want to know any. They are not the same as me. They only care about killing. The grown-ups value their own children, but they think everyone else's children have no value.

My three wishes? I have only one wish. To get well soon so I can go back to fighting the Israelis.

# Yibaneh, 18

**Kids for Kids is another name for the Youth Organization for the Recovery of Young Victims of Terrorism. It provides children affected by terrorist bombings with counseling, toys and recreation. In addition to the children who are being killed in this war, thousands on both sides have been wounded, burned, blinded, disabled and traumatized by the fighting. Kids for Kids is one of the groups that tries to help some of these children. They have a comfortable, laid-back, youth-friendly office in the Jewish Quarter of the Old City of Jerusalem.**

**Yibaneh recently lost a close friend when a Palestinian gunman opened fire at a school in the settlement where he lives. He has linked up with Kids for Kids and is helping to plan a holiday for other young people, to give them all a break from the war and from their grieving.**

I was born in Israel. I live in a settlement north of Jerusalem called Shilo. Jews have lived there for over three thousand years. It's talked about in the Bible, in the Book of Judges and in other places. It is the place where the prophet Samuel heard the word of God. The ancient ruins of the old city are still there.

The modern settlement is much newer, of course. It has a large swimming pool, a library, shops, all the normal things. A lot of writers live there, and artists, along with carpenters and many other professions. We are a small community, so we depend on each other a lot.

I have six brothers and sisters. We are all busy with school and youth groups and lots of activities.

Things have changed in Israel over the last ten years. Ten years ago, during the first Intifada, nothing much was happening. The Palestinians would throw rocks at us, but it wasn't that big a deal. Not many Israelis got killed.

Now it's different. They murdered my friend.

There's lots of shooting now on the roads. When we drive through Palestinian villages, we know that someone could shoot at us at any time. I'm used to it. I don't feel much of anything about it. When we pass a place where there has been a shooting, we'll look around, just to look, but I don't feel anything.

Several years ago there was an attempt to get a sports league going, between us and the Palestinians in the next village, but then the Intifada started, and it never happened. The Palestinians told us, "We couldn't do this now even if we wanted to. We'd be called traitors and killed by our own people."

Back then, I would have liked to play sports with the Palestinian kids. I like playing sports with anybody, so it would have been fun. I have no interest in that now. There is nothing for me to gain by trying to get to know somebody who hates me. It will only make me look weak.

I know there are good people among the Palestinians. It's impossible for a people to be all bad, every one of them. But the good people aren't talking loudly enough, or they're not being listened to, or there are not enough of them. They have leaders who are murderers, like Yasser Arafat.

I'll be going into the army soon. It's very important. The army protects our families, our friends and our country. The training will be difficult, and the things I'll have to do when I'm on duty will also be hard, but I don't think I'll mind that. At least I'll have a purpose every day.

There's a wall going up now around the West Bank. Parts of it are already up. It's supposed to keep the Palestinians away from us. I'm not sure it will help. They'll probably be able to get to us anyway.

There is no fence around my settlement. I don't think it

An Israeli police officer carries a baby to safety after a suicide bomb attack in Jerusalem.

would make a difference. We should go to war, no more peace talks. When a terrorist comes out of a village, we should go and hurt the whole village. The army tears down the houses of the suicide bombers, but that's not enough. It hasn't stopped them from killing us.

Two of my friends were killed by Palestinians. One was shot. One was killed by a bomb. Neither were in the army. They were just kids, seventeen years old. They weren't hurting anybody. They should not have died. I grew up with them. We were together all through school. Our settlement is small, only two hundred families. Everybody knows everybody. We used to do all kinds of things together. We went hiking, played sports, watched movies. They were killed just a couple of weeks ago, very close to each other. I feel sad all the time.

Their deaths make me think more about the meaning of

life in general, and the meaning of life in Israel in particular. Why am I in Israel? Is this the place for me? Is there another place? No, there isn't. This is the place where I am supposed to be. But it's not easy to see why.

God has become unclear. He's heading somewhere, but it's hard to see how this will all come to a good end.

# Wafa, 12

To discourage people from acting against Israel, the Israeli government has a policy of demolishing the family homes of Palestinian militants. Palestinian homes have also been demolished to make way for the new security wall, and to make room for expanding settlements. The homes are torn down with bulldozers and explosives.

According to UNRWA, these demolitions often occur late at night, with little or no warning. Tanks, armored personnel carriers and helicopters provide back-up for the bulldozers.

Between September 2000 and May 2003, 12,000 Palestinians became homeless when their homes were demolished. Since 1967, more than 8,000 homes have been deliberately destroyed inside Palestinian territories.

Wafa is a twelve-year-old girl who has seen her home demolished many times. Her father is a non-violent Palestinian activist who works alongside Israelis in the Israeli Committee Against House Demolitions. Israeli volunteers have helped the family rebuild their house each time the military has torn it down.

I was eight the first time my house was demolished. It was night time. My family and I were in the living room together.

Someone pounded on the door. My father opened it. There were soldiers on the other side who said, "This is not your house anymore. This is our house now."

My father said, "You are wrong. This is still my house, and I'm not going to give it to you." He shoved at the soldiers, trying to push them back outside, but there were too many of them. They hit my father on the head with their guns. He fell to the floor, and they kicked him and dragged him outside and put him under arrest.

Remains of a demolished house at a refugee camp in Ramallah.

My mother yelled and tried to get to him. She beat the soldiers with her fists. They hit her, too, very hard, so hard she had to go to the hospital.

Then the soldiers started breaking things. They fired tear gas into the house. My brothers and sisters and I couldn't breathe and had to run out into the night. The soldiers had gas masks on. We couldn't see their faces. They looked like monsters. The soldiers fire the tear gas from a sort of a gun, and it turns the air to poison. I can't breathe, my eyes cry, and my face gets very, very hot.

The soldiers dragged out everybody who was left in the house. I saw a soldier kick my little sister, who had tripped and fallen to the ground. He was yelling at her to get up or the bulldozer would run over her and crush her. I tried to get to her, but a soldier hit me with his M16 and pushed me to the ground.

A bulldozed house in a refugee camp.

Everybody got out of the house. I stood and watched as the soldiers drove the giant bulldozer into my house and destroyed it. Everything inside it was destroyed, too.

My father has lots of Israeli friends. He called them, and many Israelis came to help us rebuild our house. Before they came, I thought all Israelis were our enemies. When so many came to help us, I had to change my mind. The soldiers weren't mean to us because they are Israelis. They were mean to us because it's their job, and they enjoy it.

I learned a little bit in school about how the Israelis were treated in Germany in World War Two. The Germans killed them and put their bodies into ovens. I think the Israelis are now showing their anger at the Germans by hurting the Palestinians. I can sort of understand that, but that doesn't make it right. If I'm angry at my father, I can't beat up my brother just to make myself feel better. I don't know what the answer is, because the Israelis can't declare war on the Germans now. I don't know what would make it all right. Maybe there's nothing.

I have good memories of my house. In my bedroom there were beds and cupboards for books, toys, dolls, puzzles, games – all the normal things that children have.

I have no use for such things now. I am no longer a child, although I still like to play hide-and-seek with my friends. My best subject in school is English.

We rebuilt our house with the help of our Israeli and Palestinian friends. Just when we had it completed, the bull-dozers came again and destroyed it.

Hundreds of volunteers came to rebuild it a third time. Again the soldiers waited until the house was finished and we were ready to move in. I was very excited, because I could live in our real house again after a long time, but they destroyed it again. It is still destroyed. Volunteers are coming again in a few weeks. We will keep rebuilding the house until the Israelis get tired of destroying it and find something else to do.

I see soldiers all the time. They are everywhere. They make me afraid because I don't know what they'll do to me, or when they'll do it. They keep my town under curfew. They won't let me do the things I need to do to grow up.

Under curfew, you have to stay in the house. If you go out of the house you will be killed. Even the women. Even the children. The Israelis will shoot anybody. They don't care if you are doing anything bad or not. They will shoot you even if you look out the window. So we have to stay inside with the shutters over the windows, keeping out the sun.

Sometimes I study. Sometimes I read or watch television or

play with my brothers and sisters. We fight a lot when there is curfew. We are stuck in the apartment together, and we are bored and tired of each other, so we fight.

The soldiers use lots of different types of weapons against us. Sometimes they come with helicopters. You can hear the noise they make, especially when they come in low to try to scare us. They use gas and guns and tanks, and a kind of bomb that makes people fall over. My friends had this type of bomb thrown inside their home.

I know about children in other countries. The children in Iraq are like me. They are afraid of bombs and of being attacked. Every kid there feels the way I feel here. The kids in Europe and in the United States live in good conditions, have fun, go to school and have no curfew, but we kids in Palestine and Iraq are always afraid.

The thing I hate most are the Israelis. Not the Israelis who try to be friends with the Palestinians, but the ones who try to hurt us. I will turn this hate into action in the future. I will fight the Israelis with weapons. Palestinian women and girls are very good fighters.

I hate going through the checkpoints. The Israeli soldiers treat us like we are dogs. They make us stand and wait for no good reason, just because they can. They don't talk to us. They just ignore us, like we don't exist, like we're not even people.

Then they say, "Come!" They order us around like we are dogs. "Come!" "Stay!"

They want us to feel like we are under siege, that we can't get out. They make us wait, wait, wait, wait so long that by the time they tell us to move, I don't want to go anymore.

Killing an Israeli will make me feel glad. It will make me feel strong. I am tired of them making me feel small and weak. I want to feel strong and proud.

The Israelis will never let us have peace. We'll never have

A Palestinian boy carries books in front of his family's home after it was destroyed by Israeli tanks and bulldozers.

peace here until we have leaders, especially good Israeli leaders, not like now. Better ones. Ones who don't hate us.

My mother hasn't been well for a long time. She stopped talking. She got very, very sad each time our house was destroyed, until she was too sad to talk. I miss hearing her voice even more than I miss our house. I wanted her to talk to me so badly, to say anything, even to tell me to do something. But she couldn't. She is a little better now, and I am very grateful for that. But I am afraid that she will get really sick again.

My three wishes? I want all the Israelis who are trying to take our land to be killed. I want to be a success in my studies. This will make the Israelis nervous. They don't want us to study, and they often close our schools. And I want to build a home the soldiers can't destroy, and live in it with my family.

# Asif, 15

**The war is impossible to ignore. It affects everyone, whether you are a soldier or the loved one of a soldier, whether you are a victim or the loved one of a victim, or whether you are a taxpayer who is paying for the war. This is not an environment where people can remain neutral.**

**Asif lives in a quiet residential neighborhood of West Jerusalem with his mother, father and younger brother. The war is a frequent topic of discussion among him and his friends. They are only a few years away from performing their National Service, so what happens in the war has a real and direct effect on their future.**

I am in the tenth grade at school. My favorite subject is sports. My favorite thing to do is be with my friends and sit in coffee houses and talk.

To be Jewish in Israel means growing up faster than kids in some other countries. We have to face reality sooner, and be prepared to deal with it.

I lived in Palo Alto, California, for two years, and I noticed a big difference in the kids I knew there, and the kids I know here. There, they can live in ignorance about the world. We can't. It's not a choice we make. It's our reality. The war has made me more involved in the world.

I used to take an art class with Palestinian children. I was eleven years old. It was no big deal. They were just kids doing art, same as me. We didn't fight because they were Palestinian and I am an Israeli. We were just kids doing art.

The bombings don't make me afraid. I keep doing what I did before. Some people stay at home and hide, but that just makes them more afraid. Hiding doesn't make them safer. I'm not stupid. I keep my eyes open, but I'm not going to stop my life.

Besides, there are police and soldiers everywhere. They stop me on the street sometimes and check through my bags. It's not just me they stop. They stop a lot of people. Most buildings have guards, too. Even to get a cup of coffee, we have to be searched and go through a metal detector. We cannot forget, even for a day, where we live and what happens here.

When I'm eighteen, I'll go into the army. It's the law, for three years. Some people who don't like what Israel is doing refuse to go into the army. I won't refuse, even though I don't agree with everything they do.

For three years the army will exploit me, but I will exploit them, also. I will get the most I can out of those three years.

If I'm given an order I don't like, an order to do something I think is wrong, I will refuse to do it. It's important to protect people, protect the Palestinians, I mean. I want to be a moral voice in the army, to keep other soldiers from abusing the Palestinians. That is what my role will be.

If I were to refuse to go into the army, a military discipline board would meet to discuss my case. Almost certainly, they would put me in jail. I'd only get out of joining the army if they think I'm psychotic, but if they decide I'm psychotic, I'll never get a job. And if I do time in jail for refusing to go into the army, no one will hire me, either. But none of this matters, because I won't refuse to join. To me, that would be too easy, like running away from the problem.

It's easier for girls who don't want to serve in the military. They can do community work for their National Service.

Some people use God as an easy way to explain things. They say, "This is what God wants us to do," like "God wants us to fight this war," "God wants us to kill these people," and "God is on our side." It's an easy way to say, "I'm not responsible for what I do."

If you decide to do something, you have to live with the consequences, not God.

I hate the Israeli settlers even more than I hate the terrorists. The settlers think they are worth more as human beings than the Palestinians. They think they can push people off their land and take it over, just because they want to. They are awful people, and they make everything worse.

I don't think we'll ever get out of this situation unless we give the Palestinians their own state. It's the only way to make peace. Everyone will have to give up a little of what they want in order to get some of what they want. We're both here. Neither of us is going to go away.

I understand the suicide bombers. They do what they do because of the Israeli occupation of their land. It isn't hard to understand. We Jews did violence against the British when they controlled Israel. We killed people and blew things up in our fight for freedom. Our soldiers kill and terrorize the Palestinians, and things keep getting worse, not better. It's hard to say, "Let's make peace," to your enemy. It's easier for them to kill themselves and take some Israelis with them.

# Salam, 12

When someone commits suicide, it means they take their own life. Suicide is usually associated with despair, with the person unable to see any other way to solve their problems, and being unable to face another day in their current circumstances. People who commit suicide usually feel powerless to improve their lives.

Suicide bombers kill themselves by strapping dynamite or some other explosive material to their bodies. They then go into a public place, detonate the explosive and blow themselves up. They also blow up whoever is around them.

A number of Palestinians have killed themselves and many Israelis this way.

Many Palestinians disagree with the suicide bombings. They believe that lasting, progressive change can only come through non-violent means, and they have set up organizations to work toward strengthening the Palestinian people through education and political action. They believe the suicide bombings only give the Israeli army an excuse to engage in further oppression and hurt the reputation of the Palestinians in other countries.

But other Palestinians consider suicide bombers to be martyrs, or heroes. Their photos are posted in Palestinian towns and camps. Children collect cards and trinkets with their pictures and names. People who die as martyrs are said to have special places in paradise. Their families receive money from foreign governments as compensation. Some have summer camps named after them and are celebrated on television and in the newspapers. Before blowing themselves up, along with as many Israelis as they can, they record videotapes of themselves talking about the glory of what they are about to do.

On March 29, 2002, seventeen-year-old Aayat Al-Akhras

walked into a shoe market in West Jerusalem and blew herself up. She killed herself, a guard and a seventeen-year-old girl named Rachel Levy and wounded twenty-eight people.

Aayat's family lives in the Dheisheh refugee camp just outside Bethlehem. The camp begins off the main road on the edge of the city. There is a large tank parked in front of the Church of the Nativity, the spot where Jesus was born. Even though it will soon be Christmas, there are no pilgrims, no tourists and no citizens. Bethlehem is under curfew.

There is no barrier between the town and the camp. The buildings of the camp are separated by muddy alleys, their walls decorated with posters of Palestinian martyrs, including many posters with Aayat's picture on them. Her family's home is a square cement building on a street with many others that look just like it. The Israeli government usually destroys the home of the suicide bomber, making their family homeless, but so far, Israeli lawyers have kept this from happening to Aayat's house.

There are pictures of Aayat on every wall of the house. In the living room, a very large picture of her is in the center of a beautifully embroidered green-and-white frame.

Salam is Aayat's twelve-year-old sister.

I have six sisters and four brothers. I am in the sixth grade at school. When I grow up, I want to be a lawyer.

I am tired right now because I only went to bed a short while ago. When soldiers come, they usually come in the night, so I am too frightened to sleep then. I like to be awake at night so I am not surprised by them if they come. Being surprised by them makes it worse, makes me feel worse, more scared and ashamed.

We are under curfew now, so it doesn't matter when I sleep. We can't leave the house, so I can sleep any time I want to. I don't mind when there is a curfew because I don't like school,

Israelis protesting against their government's policies.

and there is no school when there is curfew. I don't like to study or do school work. Why bother? The Israelis won't let us do anything with our education, so why bother to get one?

I do mind that I can't see my friends and be a normal kid when there is a curfew. But if we leave the house, the soldiers will shoot at us.

I don't do anything special with my friends when we get together. We just like to be in each other's company. I get tired of being stuck inside with my brothers and sisters.

There have always been soldiers. They don't like us. I have seen the things they do. They are all around us. They throw gas bombs, shoot at children, destroy houses, arrest people and make them sit on the ground for a long time with blindfolds on. The soldiers stand over them, laughing and making them feel bad.

Of course I have been hurt by the soldiers. Everybody I know has been. I know a lot of children, smaller than me, who have been hurt by them or killed by them. I've even seen soldiers shoot at an ambulance. They don't care. They just want to kill us all.

You don't have to be doing anything bad to be hurt by the soldiers. You could just be walking down the street. I was walking down the street with my friends one day when there was no curfew, and there were some boys nearby, and the Israelis shot one of them. We all carried him to the side of the road. He didn't die. He was just shot.

When I heard that my sister had died, I was in the kitchen baking. She was late for dinner. We were all waiting for her before we ate. My parents were watching television, and we heard it on the news.

She didn't tell me she was going to do this. We shared a bedroom, but she didn't tell me.

I cried and cried.

The army came to our house that night. They smashed things. They shouted. They destroyed our door. Sarah, one of the international people, was here with us. She screamed at the soldiers to stop, but they wouldn't. They hit her just as if she had been a Palestinian. They arrested my brother. He is still in jail. He didn't do anything, but that doesn't matter to them.

We all had to go outside. They knocked us to the ground. They took my older brothers away. We had to pay a lot of money to get some of them out.

I shared a bedroom with Aayat. She was tidy, like me. One of my sisters is not tidy, and I am glad to not have to share with her. Aayat and I got along as normal children do. Sometimes we'd fight. Once she wore my shoes without asking first. That made me angry.

She spent a lot of time studying. She was better at school than I am. She always told me I should study more, but I never saw the point. I was right. Studying didn't do Aayat any good.

She didn't tell me she was going to do this. She should have told me. I would have kept her secret if she wanted me to. I would have liked to talk to her about it, maybe make her a special breakfast or do something special for her that day. She should have told me. She didn't tell any of us. She was almost finished school and was about to be married, and she kept planning those things as if everything was normal. Her fiancé is here a lot now. He is sad all the time.

I don't want you to take my picture. Someone put my picture in a big American magazine. I was crying at the time, and I don't like it that everybody in America can see me crying. So don't take my picture.

Aayat's picture is everywhere, on walls and in newspapers. She is very famous. She is a martyr and is now in paradise, where it is supposed to be very beautiful. I would like to join her there. I would have to become a martyr like her, to be able to be in paradise with her.

When I see her again in paradise, I will ask her why she didn't tell me her plans.

I don't think it would hurt if I blew myself up. I don't think it hurt my sister. I think she was very brave, not scared at all. I think she was probably very happy.

I don't know if the girl she killed had a sister my age or not. What does it matter? I don't know any Israeli kids. Why would I want to?

## Mai, 18

There are many different points of view in Israel about the Israeli relationship with the Palestinians. There are groups that call for the complete removal of Palestinians from the area, but there are also many peace groups working to increase understanding and reduce tensions.

Women in Black, a feminist organization where supportive men can also play a role, began in 1988. The concept of women in black clothing gathering in a public place to hold a silent vigil against war and injustice has since caught on around the world. Women in Black vigils are now held in Argentina, Australia, Bahrain, Canada, Colombia, Costa Rica, Denmark, Egypt, France, Germany, Ireland, Israel, Italy, Japan, Mexico, the Netherlands, Poland, Portugal, Serbia and Montenegro, Spain, Sweden, Switzerland, Turkey, the United Kingdom and the United States. Women in Black vigils have also been held in the Kashmir and some of the countries in Africa torn apart by war.

The aim of the group is to end war and violence at all levels. Some of the vigils focus on regional wars and crimes against humanity, such as mass rape and torture. Many focus on the Israeli occupation of Palestine.

The vigils are silent. Placards and banners are held, and even in the face of shouting and jeering — as often happens in Israel by people who oppose what the group stands for — the vigilers maintain a calm, dignified silence.

Mai participated in a Women in Black vigil held in downtown Jerusalem.

I am in grade twelve. I have decided not to go into the army.

My father is an actor. My mother writes and directs plays. I want to study art. Through art, we can all understand the world and each other better.

The war has affected me very much. I am very involved in politics, in activities to draw attention to the injustice that is going on, and hopefully make things better. One of the things I am doing is starting an organization called New Profile. Through it, we will talk with other young people about the army and the war.

It's very hard not to join the army. There's a lot of pressure on everyone to serve, even on girls. A lot of girls do join. They do just about everything the boys do.

It is also hard for Israelis to meet Palestinians as friends. Even though I am against the occupation, it is hard for me to have Palestinian friends. I met some Palestinians from Jenin once. We were together at a seminar in Jerusalem. They were very nice, very friendly. It is usually impossible for them to leave Jenin, because the soldiers won't let them pass the checkpoints.

I came to this vigil today to join with Women in Black in their protest, and to talk to people about New Profile. If you think something is wrong, it is important to stand up and speak out, or else everyone will think you agree with what is going on. The only way things will get better is if people speak out.

My family is supportive of my work with politics. A lot of the young people I know live in the settlements, and they do not like what I am doing. They think to have protests like this makes Israel look weak. I think it makes us look stronger, because it shows we are a strong society where differences of opinion can be expressed.

They think the Arabs should all go to other countries and leave Israel only for Jews. Not everyone in Israel thinks like that. Most people, I believe, just want peace and calm for everyone, and the easiest way to have that is to get to know each other and to just decide to get along.

When I first hear about a suicide bombing or a car bombing, I panic for two or three minutes, thinking my friends or family could be hurt. But then I just go on. It happens so often, you almost get used to it. You learn to just go on.

This war cannot last forever, but it will be a long time before we Israelis really begin to connect with the Palestinians the same way we connect with other Israelis. It's important now to stay in as close touch with the Palestinians as we can. That's the only way peace can happen. But now this wall is being built between us and them, and that will make it even harder for us to get to know each other as human beings.

I don't see God in this anywhere at all. I've never believed in God. We will make our own peace, just as we have made our own war.

Protest does work. It helps to influence the way people think. It is good to let others know what you believe. They might believe the same way, and might get the courage to say so if they see you doing it.

# FURTHER READING

*This Heated Place: Encounters in the Promised Land*
Deborah Campbell, Douglas and McIntyre, 2002.
This beautifully written book for adults can easily be read by young adults. It describes the author's travels and conversations in Israel and Palestine.

*Samir and Yonatan*
Daniella Carmi, Scholastic, 2002.
A novel for young readers about a Palestinian boy awaiting surgery in an Israeli hospital. Ages 10 to 14.

*Children of Israel, Children of Palestine: Our Own True Stories*
Laurel Holliday, Washington Square Press, 1999.
Children talk about their lives in Israel and Palestine. Ages 13 and up.

*Why Do They Hate Me? Young Lives Caught in War and Conflict*
Laurel Holliday, Simon and Schuster, 1999.
Excerpts from the diaries of young people living in times of war, including World War II, Northern Ireland and Israel/Palestine. Gives insight into what it is like to be a child in a place of war. Ages 13 and up.

*A Small Patch of Ground*
Elizabeth Laird, Macmillan, 2002.
A remarkable young adult novel about a Palestinian boy who wants to be a football star. Ages 13 and up.

*Number the Stars*
Lois Lowry, Yearling, 1990.
A novel about a ten-year-old girl and the Danish resistance to the Nazis. Ages 10 to 14.

*Habibi*
Naomi Shihab Nye, Simon and Schuster, 1997.
The story of a fourteen-year-old girl who moves from Missouri to Jerusalem. Ages 10 to 14.

*Occupied Voices: Stories of Everyday Life from the Second Intifada*
Wendy Pearlman, Thunder's Mouth Press, 2003.
First-person accounts of Palestinians living in the occupied territories, including some interviews with children. Written for adults, but very accessible for younger readers.

*To Cross a Line*
Karen Ray, Orchard Books, 1994.
A novel based on the true story of a seventeen-year-old Jewish boy's escape from Nazi Germany. Ages 13 and up.

*The Hopscotch Tree*
Leda Siskind, Bantam, 1992.
A novel about a girl dealing with anti-Semitism in America. Ages 9 to 11.

*Israel/Palestine: How to End the War of 1948*
Tanya Reinhart, Seven Stories Press, 2002.
An adult non-fiction book that provides a good historical overview of the war and the consequences of the ongoing occupation.

# ORGANIZATIONS

Below is a very short list of some of the many organizations trying to make a difference in the situation in Israel and Palestine.

Givat Haviva
M.P. Menashe 37850, Israel
www.dialogate.org.il
Winner of the 2001 UNESCO Prize for Peace Education, this organization brings together Palestinians and Israelis.

*Crossing Borders*
The International People's College, Elsinore, Denmark
www.crossingborder.org
A bi-monthly youth magazine with Palestinian, Israeli, Jordanian and Arab-Israeli contributors.

Israeli Committee Against House Demolitions (ICAHD)
P.O. Box 2030, Jerusalem 91020, Israel
www.icahd.org
An organization helping Palestinians whose homes are under threat of demolition by the Israeli army.

Gush Shalom
P.O. Box 3322, Tel Aviv 61033, Israel
www.gush-shalom.org
An Israeli peace organization.

Kids for Kids
16/4 Tiferet Israel St., Old City, Jerusalem 97500, Israel
www.kidsforkids.net
An Israeli organization providing support and recreation for Israeli kids traumatized by the war.

Hamoked, Center for the Defence of the Individual
4 Abu Obeidah Street, Jerusalem 97200, Israel
www.hamoked.org.il
A human rights organization.

International Solidarity Movement
info@palsolidarity.org
www.palsolidarity.org
This organization sends international observers into Palestinian territories to monitor the situation and act as advocates for Palestinian individuals when possible.

Christian Peacemakers
Box 72063, 1562 Danforth Avenue, Toronto, Ontario, Canada M4J 1N4
www.cpt.org
An organization that sends international observers to war zones around the world, including Palestine.

# ACKNOWLEDGMENTS

I would like to express my appreciation to all the Israelis and Palestinians who took the time to talk with me and let me share in their lives and work. I would also like to thank Oded Haklai, Paul Kingston, Richard Swift and my editor, Shelley Tanaka.

**Deborah Ellis** is the author of *The Breadwinner, Parvana's Journey* and *Mud City*, which have sold hundreds of thousands of copies in seventeen languages. Her books have won Sweden's Peter Pan Prize, the Rocky Mountain Book Award, the Ruth Schwartz Award, the University of California's Middle East Book Award and the Jane Addams' Peace Award. Deb is also the author of *A Company of Fools* and *Looking for X*, which won the Governor General's Award for Children's Literature.